NUKE-REBUKE

The Spirit That Moves Us Press books are distributed to bookstores directly and thru Bookslinger, Bookpeople, Small Press Distribution, Inland Book Company, The Distributors, and Writers & Books. Selected titles are available also thru The Small Press Book Club (Dustbooks).

Libraries may order directly or thru Baker & Taylor (their Approval Program), Blackwell North America, Midwest Library Service and many other jobbers.

Individuals are encouraged to ask their local bookstores to order what they don't have in stock, or they may order directly from us.

Teachers: We have a bulk order (ten or more copies) discount, and you receive a free desk copy.

New Subscription Structure:
Libraries and individuals may subscribe in two ways—
1) serially, beginning with any issue/book (minimum of 2), cost based on 25% off the cover prices;
2) any combination of issues/books (minimum of 2), 20% off cover prices.   In either case, postage is paid by us.
Libraries may subscribe directly or thru EBSCO, Faxon and many others.
Subscriptions may be in perfectbound or cloth editions, where both editions are available.
Send for our catalog.

The Spirit That Moves Us (ISBN prefix 0-930370; ISSN 0364-4014) is indexed in *Index of American Periodical Verse; Index to Periodical Fiction;* and *The American Humanities Index*. Both *The Actualist Anthology* and *Editor's Choice* have been indexed in *Granger's Index to Poetry*.

Most of what is published by The Spirit That Moves Us comes to us unsolicited, but please send a s.a.s.postcard to determine our current needs.

In Print:
Editor's Choice: Literature & Graphics from the U.S. Small Press, 1965-1977;
The Spirit That Moves Us Reader;   The Farm In Calabria, by David Ray;
The Casting Of Bells, by Jaroslav Seifert;   *The Actualist Anthology;*
Here's The Story: Contemporary Fiction With A Heart (Spring 1984);
The Poem You Asked For, by Marianne Wolfe;   *Riverside,* by Morty Sklar;
Cross-Fertilization: The Human Spirit As Place (anthology: poetry & fict.);
Editor's Choice II: Poetry & Fiction from the U.S. Small Press, 1978-1983
(November 1984);   All issues of the magazine (from 1975) are in print.

NUKE-REBUKE:

WRITERS & ARTISTS AGAINST NUCLEAR ENERGY & WEAPONS

Edited by Morty Sklar

Poetry / Fiction / Essays / Artwork

This book should be considered by
subscribers to *The Spirit That Moves Us*
as Volume 7, Number 1.

The Spirit That Moves Us Press
P.O. Box 1585, Iowa City, Iowa 52244

Acknowledgements & Other Information

(Where a slash appears, it should be taken to mean *first appeared in.*)
Don Dolan's artwork/his *The Last Days Of The American Dream* (Fault Press). Thanks to John W. Dower for making us aware of Kyoko and Mark Selden, from whom Hayashi Kyoko's story was obtained. Dan Sullivan's photo/*Luna Tack*. Gary Snyder's "Strategic Air Command"/his *Axe Handles* (North Point Press, 1983). Marge Piercy's "The Track Of The Master Builder"/her *Circles On The Water* (Alfred A. Knopf, 1982). D. Nurkse's "Lamps And Fences"/*Pulpsmith*; his "Closed Borders"/*Stone Country*. Jascha Kessler's "Teiresias"/*Chelsea*. W.D. Ehrhart's "Sunset"/his *The Samisdat Poems* (Samisdat Press). William Stafford's "Incident"/*Slow Loris Reader*. David Ray's "An Old Woodcut"/*Chariton Review*. William Pitt Root's "The Day The Sun Rises Twice"/*Meltdown: Poems From The Core* (Full Count Press). Brown Miller's "It's Hour Come Round At Last"/his *Hiroshima Flows Through Us* (Cherry Valley Editions). Morty Sklar's "Poem To The Sun"/*New Letters*, and was anthologized in *A to Z: 200 Contemporary American Poets* (Swallow Press/Ohio Univ. Press). David Hilton's "1952"/*The Cincinnati Review*. Floyd Skloot's "Rules Of The Game"/*The Chowder Review*. Tam Lin Neville's "Grief Dance From A Distant Place"/*Epos*. Warren Woessner's "Looking At Power"/*Beloit Poetry Journal*, and was included in his *No Hiding Place* (Spoon River Press). Curt Johnson's "Our Nuclear Future"/*Science Experimenter*. Thanks to: the Educational Fdn. for Nuclear Science for permission to excerpt *The Final Epidemic* for our "By Way Of A Preface"; the Iowa Historical Society for permission to publish their photo; the Hiroshima-Nagasaki Publishing Committee (Japan) for permission to reprint photos from their *Days To Remember*, and to Barbara Yates for sending it to us.

Gratitude is also expressed to the following for grants, or donations of cash or services:
The National Endowment for the Arts, a federal agency, for a matching grant.
The Iowa Arts Council, for a matching grant.
Technigraphics; H.J. Heinz Co.; Jim Gilmore; Iowa State Bank; Norma Vogel; Selma Sklar; Richard Winter; Soap Opera; Herteen & Stocker; C.A.C.; Anonymous; Bill Gauger; Gilda Imports; Frohwein Office Supplies; Dain Bosworth, Inc.

*

Copyright © 1984 by The Spirit That Moves Us Press, Inc. (rights revert to contributors)
First Edition, clothbound & perfectbound, 1984.
Number 5 of The Contemporary Anthology Series
Printed by McNaughton & Gunn
*

Library of Congress Cataloging in Publication Data
Main entry under title:

Nuke-rebuke : writers & artists against nuclear energy & weapons.

(The Contemporary anthology series ; v. 5)
1. Atomic weapons and disarmament—Literary collections. 2. Atomic power industry—Literary collections.
3. Antinuclear movement—Literary collections.
4. Peace—Literary collections. 5. American literature
—20th century. I. Sklar, Morty, 1935-
II. Series.
PS509.A85N84   1984   810'.8'0358   83-20140
ISBN 0-930370-16-3
ISBN 0-930370-17-1 (pbk.)
ISBN 0-930370-15-0 (signed A-Z)

"... this most meager provision,
your life."
—Robert Creeley

"For we have forgotten this: that the Earth is a star of grass..."
—Rolf Jacobsen

Sedako's cranes are flying
hovering
seeking a resting-place

Sedako's cranes are flying
hovering
seeking a resting-place
in our hearts

Sedako's cranes are crying
a thousand cranes are crying
pleading:
"Keep the dream of peace
in your hearts."

This is our cry,
this is our prayer:
peace to the world.

—Dennis Brutus

5

Introduction

COVER LETTERS accompanying most manuscripts sent for consideration for this collection were sparked with enthusiasm or/and concern. Excerpted from David Hilton's letter: "It begins to seem as if we live in an age when for the first time in human history there exists reified the *ultimate cause*—the perpetuation of the human race, or true humanism." Whereas in the past, life was sometimes a struggle and sometimes not, life for the most part was a given. Now there is the possibility of not just parts of the world being laid to ruin, but all of it; not just the fall of another empire, but of civilization and all of life itself.

I imagine that when you, Reader, saw the title of this book you might have expected the contents to lean strongly toward the "militant," the polemical, and perhaps the rhetorical and humorless. And maybe you suspected that ideas and conviction would prevail at the expense of effective and artful expression. As you will see, that is not the case. "Radical" (as tho concern for human life is not central to most political persuasions) and scientific work abound, but someone else can do a better job of collecting work of that kind. What I've aimed for here is a personal kind of expression, and work which not only expresses concern for life and living, but does so with the artist's skill. Even the scientific excerpts in "By Way Of A Preface" emphasize the personal: the impossibility, for instance, of dealing just with burn victims in the event of a nuclear attack; and the infinitesimal cost (in relation to military spending) of cleaning up Earth's drinking water, the impurity of which is the cause of most disease in underdeveloped countries.

Various perspectives of the contents: Hayashi Kyoko's long story centers around her experience as a young schoolgirl caught in the Nagasaki bombing, and is an odyssey thru the Valley of the Shadow of Death. It seems that since the horror of the bombing and its aftermath was so great and known both personally and indirectly to so many people, her expression tends to be almost flat as if to counterpoint the reality, with only occasional exclamations... and yet it sings like a high-voltage wire strung serenely from pole to pole over a great expanse. David Ray's poem about Harry Truman expresses anger and moral indignation in a more head-on way. Don Dolan's surrealistic war scenarios are not necessarily about nuclear war, but in their fierceness tell us that all war is inhuman. Others are gentler in their approaches to the horrors of what has already happened and the fears of what could happen: Margaret Randall in her poem about her twelve-year-old daughter who is in army fatigues one day and experimenting with makeup the next, in a country at war—Nicaragua; Judith Waring in her personal account of a family caught in the confusion of the Three Mile Island malfunction; Byron Burford in his painting of women making bullets in an old factory, looking as at ease or bored or domestic or industrious as women—or men—doing just about anything; Diane Glancy in her poem of the American Indian tradition of asking a bear its permission to kill it. Jacques Prevert's poem has nothing to do, directly, with the theme of this book, but it does have to do with the humorless, regimental forming of young minds—and the mind which won't be molded. Grace Shinell's story is a speculation on the aftermath of a nuclear holocaust, related in a neo-scientific, inadvertently humorous style by an historian of a land east of the North American continent. I will risk redundancy by saying that Tom Hansen's found poem, "Complaint," is included because so much attention in this court record is paid to the details of a single person's death by murder, whereas the thought of sudden and long-term obliteration of life as the result of nuclear attack or war tends to view life and death as an abstract concept.

I would like to pay tribute to some of the luck which has befallen me in the making of this book (other acknowledgements are made on page four): My having chosen to see a slide show of Nagasaki-Hiroshima art, shown by John Dower on an evening when I'd already planned to go to a poetry reading, and thus in a roundabout way coming to discover the Hayashi Kyoko story; my friend Barbara Yates' having sent me from Japan, an unsolicited pamphlet called "Days To Remember," from which some photographs are reprinted here; being at Gary Snyder's reading in Iowa City, where he granted permission to publish his "Strategic Air Command"—just in time for my being able to reduce the size of the typeface for the contributor notes, so that the already-typeset *Nuke-Rebuke* could accommodate the poem.

I also appreciated the response of the WOPR (War Operations Plan Response) computer in the film "War Games," following its playout of the Global Thermonuclear War game: "Strange game. The only winning move is not to play."

—Morty Sklar
in the heartland/December 24, 1983

7

By Way Of A Preface

The following is gleaned, with permission, from The Final
Epidemic: Physicians and Scientists on Nuclear War, *edited
by Ruth Adams and Susan Cullen, and published by the
Educational Foundation for Nuclear Science.*

From the Introduction, by Helen Caldicott:
  The World is moving rapidly toward the final medical epidemic, thermonuclear war. This planet can be compared to a
terminally ill patient infected with lethal "macrobes" which
are metastasizing rapidly. The terminal event will be essential-
ly medical in nature, but there will be few physicians remaining to treat the survivors.
  In the past, incurable epidemics of bacterial or viral disease
have been controlled or eliminated by preventive medicine.
The lessons of preventive medicine apply equally to the most
serious event threatening to befall the human race—nuclear
war. It can be averted by a concerted and urgent campaign
conducted by physicians throughout the world, united by an
allegiance to the ancient Hippocratic oath.

From Chapter 3, by Victor Sidel, the "Symptoms" section:
  As the Council for a Livable World and other groups have
pointed out, military expenditures are themselves destructive
of human life, even if the weapons we stockpile are never used.
The diversion of a large part of the world's resources to prep-
aration for war leaves far less available for health services and
for other efforts that would improve the duration and the
quality of life of the world's peoples.
  We need not wait for the ultimate horror—the "last epidemic"—that nuclear war represents. Preventable endemic and epidemic disease, hunger, misery and premature death surround
us now, in the midst of a potentially productive and bountiful world. Much of the world's illness, particularly in developing countries, could be prevented or ameliorated by the redirection of a fraction of the resources that the world diverts to
arms.
  The massive arms investment in the United States and in a

number of other countries has diverted capital from the modernization of productive capacity for the civilian economy. Countries such as Japan, and until recently, West Germany, which spent far less on arms, have far surpassed the United States in their rate of growth in manufacturing productivity. Expansion of health and other human services depends largely on an expanding "economic pie." If the pie is not increasing, it is harder to convince people, and their political representatives, to increase the amount spent on publicly-funded services for the underserved.

An editorial entitled "Burning $1 Trillion" in the January 22, 1980 *Wall Street Journal* said that "Defense spending is the worst kind of government outlay," because it not only increases income without increasing the supply of goods that consumers can buy but it also "eats up materials and other resources that otherwise could be used to produce consumer goods."

Expenditures for military production create far fewer jobs than expenditures for human services. When the United States spends $1 billion on arms, for example, it creates some 40,000 jobs; the same amount spent on nursing creates some 80,000 jobs. Furthermore, since many health insurance programs are tied to employment, unemployment often terminates health insurance coverage.

Edward F. Snyder of the Friends Committee on National Legislation, in his testimony on the 1979 federal budget before the House Budget Committee: "Six surveillance and command planes added for an additional cost of $120 million; Headstart programs (pre-school training) cut $20 million.... One submarine tender to support nuclear attack submarines added for an additional $262.5 million; maternal and child health services cut $112 million .... An additional $89 million for the Army XM-1 tank program; mental health centers cut $88 million .... An additional $141 million for A-10 attack aircraft; cancer research cut $55 million."

The entire annual budget of $20 million for the U.S. Public Health Service Hospital in Seattle, scheduled to close in 1982, is less than two-thirds the cost of one AH-64 military helicopter.

The total cost of the program that eradicated smallpox from the Earth is less than the cost of six hours of the world arms race.

From Chapter 17, by Bernard Lown, in "Treatment" section:
The lack of clean water accounts for 80 percent of all the world's illness. With a diversion of funds consumed by three weeks of the arms race, the world could obtain a sanitary water supply for all of its inhabitants.

From Chapter 5, by Evgeni I. Chazov, in "Causes" section:
Humanity is now sitting on a powder keg which holds 10 tons of TNT for each one of us.

In the developing countries today, 100 million children are in danger of dying because of malnutrition and vitamin short-age, and 30 percent of the children have no possibility of go-ing to school. Yet military expenditures world wide are 20 to 25 times bigger than the total aid provided annually to the de-veloping countries by the developed states. For example, in the past ten years the World Health Organization spent about $83 million on smallpox eradication—less than the cost of one modern strategic bomber. According to some World Health Organization calculations, $450 million are needed to eradi-cate malaria, a disease which affects over one billion people in 66 countries of the world. This is less than half of what is spent in the world on arms every day.

From Chapter 12, by Howard H. Hiatt, in "Prognosis" section:
In the aftermath of a nuclear attack on Boston, what are the prospects for medical care? Using as their base a figure of 6,560 physicians in the Boston metropolitan area at the time of attack, the 1959 and 1962 studies project that almost 5,000 will be killed immediately or fatally injured, and that only 900 will be in condition to render post-attack medical care. The ration of injured persons to physicians is thus in ex-cess of 1,700 to one. If a physician spends an average of only 15 minutes with each injured person and works 16 hours each day, the studies project, it will take from 16 to 26 days for each casualty to be seen once.

If we examine the consequences of nuclear war in medical terms, we must pay heed to the inescapable lesson of contemporary medicine: where treatment of a given disease is ineffective *or* where costs are insupportable, attention must be given to prevention. Both conditions apply to the effects of nuclear war—treatment programs would be virtually useless and the costs would be staggering.

From Chapter 13, by H. Jack Geiger, in "Prognosis" section:
In San Francisco, the U.S. Arms Control and Disarmament Agency calculates that a single one-megaton air burst would kill 624,000 persons and seriously injure and incapacitate 306,000 .... Among "survivors" there will probably be tens of thousands of cases of extensive third-degree burns. And in this kind of injury, survival and recovery depend almost entirely on the availability of specialized burn-care facilities, highly and specially trained medical and allied personnel, complex laboratory equipment, almost unlimited supplies of blood and plasma, and the availability of a wide range of drugs. No such facilities would remain intact in San Francisco; the number of Bay Area burn casualties would exceed by a factor of 10 or 20 the capacity of all the burn-care centers in the United States.

In addition to third-degree burns, hundreds of thousands of "survivors" would suffer crushing injuries, simple and compound fractures, penetrating wounds of the skull, thorax and abdomen, and multiple lacerations with extensive hemorrhage, primarily in consequence of blast pressures and the collapse of buildings. (Many of these victims, of course, would also have serious burns.) A moderate number would have ruptured internal organs, particularly the lungs, from blast pressures. Significant numbers would be deaf in consequence of ruptured eardrums, in addition to their other injuries, and many would be blind, since—as far as 35 miles from ground zero—reflex glance at the fireball would produce serious retinal burns.

Superimposed on these problems would be tens of thousands of cases of acute radiation injury, superficial burns produced by beta and low-energy gamma rays, and damage due to radionucleides in specific organs. Many would die even if the most sophisticated and heroic therapy were available; others, with similar symptoms but less actual exposure, could be saved by skilled and complex treatment. In practical terms, however, there will be no way to distinguish the lethally-irradiated from the non-lethally-irradiated.

These are the short-range problems to which a medical response must be addressed. But who will be left to respond?

And all of this is happening in an area where there is no electricity, no surviving transportation system. What is left of the buildings is lying in what is left of the streets; the bridges are down; subways and tunnels are crushed; there is no effective communication system; there are no ambulances and no hospitals.

Finally, in each ten-minute patient visit, the "medical care" will be dispensed without x-rays, laboratory equipment, other diagnostic aids, supplies, drugs, blood, plasma, beds and the like. There will be no help from "outside." There will be no rational organization even of this primitive level of care. In short, this is not medical care at all, as we commonly understand it.

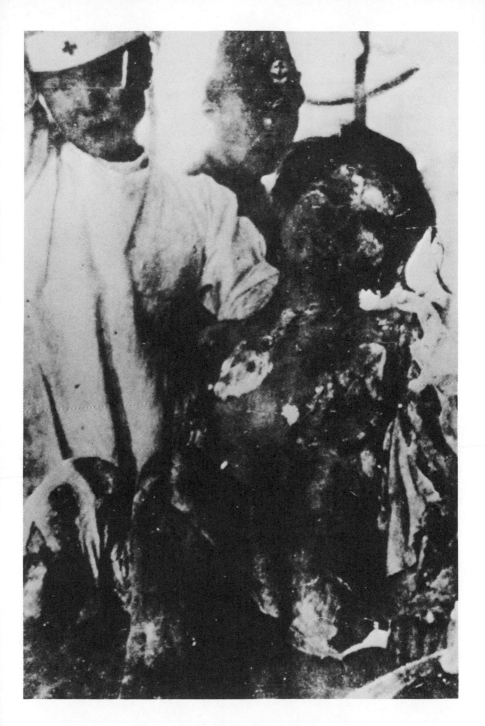

Anonymous / Nagasaki photo / from *Days To Remember*

CONTENTS

16

Alphabetical Listing Of Contributors

Jimmy Santiago Baca
Daniel Berrigan
James Bertolino
John Brandi
Joseph Bruchac
Dennis Brutus
Byron Burford
Grant Burns
Robert M. Chute
Michael Clark
Robert Creeley
Cathy Young Czapla
Hank De Leo
Don Dolan
W.D. Ehrhart
Sally Fisher
Hugh Fox
Robert Franzini
Diane Glancy
James Grabill
Chael Graham (transl.)
Roger Greenwald (transl.)

Tom Hansen
Dellas Henke
David Hilton
Will Inman
Rolf Jacobsen
Curt Johnson
Terrance Keenan
Jascha Kessler
Hayashi Kyoko
Daniel J. Langton
Cleveland Latham
Eugene McCarthy
Brown Miller
David Mura
Tam Lin Neville
D. Nurkse
William Oandasan
Lee Patton
Peter Payack
Marge Piercy
Carlo Pittore
Jacques Prevert

Margaret Randall
David Ray
Helen Redman
Gay Rogers
William Pitt Root
Randall W. Scholes
Hillel Schwartz
Kyoko Selden (transl.)
Grace Shinell
Layle Silbert
Morty Sklar
Floyd Skloot
Gary Snyder
William Stafford
Robert Stewart
Dan Sullivan
Judith Waring
Candice Warne
A.D. Winans
Warren Woessner
Yamahata Yosuke

17

Gary Snyder
STRATEGIC AIR COMMAND

The hiss and flashing lights of a jet
Pass near Jupiter in Virgo.
He asks, how many satellites in the sky?
Does anyone know where they all are?
What are they doing, who watches them?

Frost settles on the sleeping bags.
The last embers of fire,
One more cup of tea,
At the edge of a high lake rimmed with snow.

These cliffs and the stars
Belong to the same universe.
This little air in between
Belongs to the twentieth century and its wars.

VIII, 82, Koip Peak, Sierra Nevada

Yamahata Yosuke / Nagasaki photo

Hayashi Kyoko
RITUAL OF DEATH

THE DEVICE that was dropped over Nagasaki to record the force of the blast produced by the atomic bomb contained a letter calling for surrender. It was addressed to Professor Sagane of Tokyo University, and was signed by three fellow scientists whom Professor Sagane had known while studying in the United States.

Displayed at the "Hiroshima-Nagasaki Atomic Bomb Exhibit" the letter reads:

August 9, 1945

To Professor R. Sagane

From three of your former scientific colleagues during your stay in the United States.

We are sending this as a personal message to urge that you use your influence as a reputable nuclear physicist to convince the Japanese General Staff of the terrible consequences which will be suffered by your people if you continue in this war.

Within the space of three weeks we have proof-fired on land in the American desert, exploded one in Hiroshima, and fired the third this morning.

We implore you to confirm these facts to your leader, and to do your utmost to stop the destruction and waste of life which can only result in the total annihilation of all your cities, if continued. As scientists, we deplore the use to which a beautiful discovery has been put, but we can assure you that unless Japan surrenders at once, this rain of atomic bombs will increase manyfold in fury.

It is impossible for me to read this letter calmly, for I was exposed to the atomic bomb in Nagasaki. The effect of the warning, coming after the bombing, was designed to be heightened by the sacrifice of the lives of people I knew.

It is particularly painful to read of "this rain of atomic bombs" which "will increase manyfold in fury," and take it simply as a statement of events to come. I recall Urakami on August 9, when the shower of the atomic bomb raged down violently and killed my friends. I admire those three scientists who could write that letter so matter-of-factly—or the U. S. government which made them write it—secure that they could justly rage because they were children of God.

Another passage makes me ponder. The letter says, "a third atomic bomb was dropped this morning," but purposely—so that Fate might intervene—leaving blank the projected target of the bomb. It is easy to imagine that there were several alternate targets, that Nagasaki was not necessarily doomed from the start, especially if the purpose of the letter

21

was to stop the war. And yet Nagasaki was unfortunate enough to be chosen. In fact, according to the description in the same letter of the procedure before the bombing in Hiroshima and Nagasaki, Field Operations Order Number 17 of August 8th made Kokura the main target, and Nagasaki only an alternative. At 2:49 a.m., August 9, a B-29 loaded with an atomic bomb, accompanied by another B-29, left Tinian Air Base and headed for Kokura.

When they reached Kokura, they could not see the city because of thick clouds. They circled three times, and, fearing loss of fuel, flew on to Nagasaki, the alternate site.

The point is that the relative visibility through the clouds divided the fates of Nagasaki and Kokura. The B-29s quietly flew over serene Chijiwa Bay by way of the Shimabara peninsula and into Nagasaki, arriving over the city at 10:58. It was cloudy there too, registering 8 on the cloud scale. It registers 10 if the entire sky is covered with clouds. But the scale does not measure the thickness of the clouds, and although the letter says that visibility was very poor, a different source records: "August 9, windless and fair." Diaries of some who experienced the bombing also say, "fair," or "very fair." According to my memory, it was hot and clear. At least the clouds in the upper sky were not thick enough to produce a cloudy day on the earth.

The first of the two B-29s parachuted a measuring device. Then the bombardier glimpsed the Nagasaki Iron Foundry through the clouds and instantly pushed the button. The foundry was located in Hamaguchimachi near Urakami Station. At 11:02 the bomb, attached to a white parachute, exploded in the sky 490 meters above the ground in Matsuyama-machi. There had been an air raid siren around ten in the morning, but at the time of the explosion the warning had been withdrawn.

Some students of N Girls' High School, including myself, were then at work at the Ohashi Factory of the Mitsubishi Munitions Plant, 1.4 kilometers from the center of the bombing. We worked at the north end of the factory lot. The official death rate in this area was 45.5 percent. But 6,200 of the 7,500 people who worked in that plant, including mobilized students and regular workers, were not included in the calculation. According to a survey conducted as late as September 24, 1945, their whereabouts were unknown. We do not know for sure if they are dead or alive, but they are almost certainly dead. If these people are included, the death rate was much higher than 45.5 percent. The Mitsubishi Munitions Plant of Nagasaki closed on November 15, 1945.

Whether it was Kokura or Nagasaki, we in the city whose name went unmentioned in the letter quoted above lived our lives unaware that this "rain of atomic bombs" would rage more violently. Most of us did not even know why that rage should be directed toward us, and we thought we were going to live tomorrow and the day after tomorrow. Some stared open-mouthed at the atomic bomb wafting down under an open parachute from the sky, unaccompanied by an air raid siren, thinking that it probably was food for the American captives. I think it was either Hamaguchi-machi or Matsuyama-machi, but near the railway tracks going to Ohashi, American prisoners lived surrounded by a wire fence. Inside the tall wire netting, like the nets around a golf driving range, they were constantly digging. They did not grow vegetables. Maybe they were building a trench. Whatever they were doing, they always dug with shovels. When we chanced to pass by during one recess, they watched us go, twining their white fingers around the wire. Their blue and gray eyes looked friendly as they followed Japanese people walking in freedom. They looked around twenty years old. On August 9, did they also die in the atomic bombing? If they had been at work as usual, they must have died—a glorious death in action. What kind of letters reported their deaths to their bereaved families?

Isahaya is a castle town twenty-five kilometers from Nagasaki. It is the sixth station from Nagasaki, past Urakami, Michi-no-O, Nagayo, Okusa, and Kigitsu, and one hour's ride on the Nagasaki Honsen Railway. My mother and sisters lived in Isahaya then. It was near the mouth of the Honmyo River, and it had a salty smell from the Ariake Sea.

My father worked for a firm overseas and was not home. I lived in a boarding house in Nagasaki. N Girls' High School was located in Nishiyama, Nagasaki. It belonged to the same neighborhood association as the Suwa Shrine, and across the street from school was the Nagasaki Business High School. The direct distance from the center of the bombing is three kilometers.

The students were mobilized to work in factories beginning in May of that year, the season when the sunlight is fairest in Nagasaki, and when the green of the trees seems to color the stone steps.

On August 9, at ten in the morning, my mother and younger sister went to work in the field. They had a small garden on top of the hill to the right of the bus road along the Honmyo River, where they grew ten short rows of vegetables. My mother had planted sweet potatoes because they were easy for amateurs. There was a fine view from the hill that day, and the Navy Hospital and Isahaya Station upstream were clearly visible.

"Be careful not to hurt the roots," my mother said to my little sister as she put her fingers into the dirt. Sweet potatoes in August were thin, like the thumb of a grown-up. They were called miniature potatoes, and used as offerings to the dead. They were too precious to eat.

Thrusting her fingers into the well-tilled, soft earth, my mother pulled out a miniature potato very carefully so that she would not hurt the other roots. She only needed about ten, so she did not have to struggle with the hoe. But since she had to dig them out one by one, it took time. The salty wind blew up from the river and the Ariake Sea, and it was cool in the morning light. Toward noon, when the sun shone right above, it grew hot. The slightly reddish sweet potato leaves drooped; the earth heated; their bodies felt steaming.

My little sister, who was a fourth-grader, grew tired and pulled at my mother's *mompe* trousers, "Let's go home," she said. My mother glanced at her watch, originally gold plated, but now, in tune with wartime austerity, recovered with chrome. It was eleven.

She stood up, holding the sieveful of miniature potatoes. At that moment, the surface of the river winding at the foot of the hill sparkled for a second, and a white light spread from the direction of Kigitsu, crawling up under the sky.

"Mother, something flashed!" my sister shouted.

The radiance did not draw sharp lines like lightning, but covered the sky slowly, like the light of flare bombs, and disappeared.

There were no clouds in the sky of Isahaya, and the sun was shining brightly. In the added brightness the hills and the river at midday became sheer white. Then a great noise shook the earth—the heavy thunder of an explosion. Several minutes later, dust-filled wind whipped across my mother's face.

The leaves of the sweet potatoes were blown down in the furrows and then flew up showing their white undersides. My mother grabbed the sieve and my sister's arm and ran down the footpath that divided the fields. The air raid must be in Kigitsu, she thought. It can't be as far as Okusa, with all this noise and wind. She looked up while running, and saw burning red around the sun and black spots the size of flies moving toward her. The ridge of the Kigitsu mountains was etched with blackish red clouds, which were gradually swelling.

"Run back and tell your uncle. I think Kigitsu's been hit."

The only son of my mother's elder brother lived in a lodging house in Kigitsu. He had just entered the Nagasaki Medical School. Kigitsu is a quiet village surrounded by the sea, and by mountains planted with orange trees. It was a good place to study. Our cousin rented a room and commuted to school from there.

When my mother got to the bus road, a crowd was gathering, shocked by the strange flash. A huge pillar of cloud hung in the sky, the bottom of it deep red.

"What can that be?" Pointing at the cloud, my mother asked a middle-aged man wearing a helmet. "I don't know, it's weird," he answered, his eyes glued to the cloud. A peasant with a spade on his shoulder said, "It looks like Kigitsu is burning."

Nobody even imagined that Nagasaki, twenty-five kilometers away, was burning. In the afternoon, my sister, who had been playing outside in the field came home and showed my mother a piece of crepe cloth with a wisteria pattern. "What a funny thing, it fell from the sky," she said. It looked like a piece forcibly torn from a woman's kimono. Since it was impossible for a piece of cloth like that to fall from the sky, my mother listened only halfheartedly.

"A lot of newspapers floated over from the mountains of Kigitsu, too," my sister said, waving her hands, my mother listening in silence. "This came flying down too," she said and held up a stick of wood about thirty centimeters long. My mother took it and examined it. It was a piece of a varnished picture frame. The brush and ink writing on it said "Nagasaki." Where the black writing had been, the wood was charred, there was a date on it, probably of a photograph. The cloth and stick both flew from Nagasaki on the wind created in the explosion. It carried the wisteria cloth twenty-five kilometers. Who was wearing that kimono, and where in the city was she walking?

The greatest registered natural wind velocity is 70 meters per second. At 0.5 kilometers from the center of the attack, the velocity of the wind generated by the atomic bomb is estimated to have been 360 meters per second, comparable to the speed of sound. (The Ise Bay typhoon of 1959 that hit the coast of Nagoya carried winds of 45 meters per second.) Human flesh exposed to a wind of that velocity would be torn off. The measuring device that had been dropped from the observation plane was found near Matsubara-cho, Isahaya.

The black rain, later to be called the "rain of death," fell on Isahaya as elsewhere. It had lethal or crippling radioactive elements, and while my mother was washing the miniature potatoes at the well, two or three hours after the explosion, it fell on her arms and neck. More than rain, it fell like mist from a sprayer. At that point, we all thought it was weird because it was black; beyond that nobody gave it much thought. It was only after the war that people began to call it the black rain, or the rain of death, and made a fuss about it. My mother was no exception. She didn't even notice that her laundry was sprinkled with it, so she folded the clothes and put them away.

A few days later when people had started to talk about the new type of bomb, she took out some of the clothes and discovered that the black rain had made spots on them, like mildew during the rainy season. Did the dark spots floating near the sun turn into black raindrops? My mother took the clothes out to the yard and burnt them. It was too bad, because things were scarce in those days, but the black rain spots looked like human blood. The atomic bomb killed 73,889 people in an instant. Even now when the rain is explained as radioactive dust, my mother still says: "They were bloodstains."

In the late afternoon of the same day, rumor circulated that it was neither Kigitsu nor Okusa but Nagasaki that had been bombed. Before my sister reached our uncle, my mother's elder brother, he had already set out hurriedly to Kigitsu on his rusty bike to find out if his son was safe. He returned at about five o'clock, a look of relief on his face, and reported the safety of Kigitsu, saying, "The orange trees were all right, and the houses, too." Kigitsu was an orange-growing area next to Okusa. Peeling one of the summer oranges he had brought back, he said, "He had gone to school, though." Then after a silence, he added that Nagasaki seemed to have been hit, and sank into thought.

"Nagasaki is a big city. Besides, the medical school and the munitions plant could stand up against a bomb," my mother said, and was not worried about me, working in the plant.

Students who worked there had been told to take shelter at a warning siren in the trenches in the hill at the back of the factory. The shelter for N Girls' High School was a trench dug into a slope that was covered with cedar trees. Its entrance was covered with moss, and inside water dripped. But it went deep inside the hill and seemed secure. I had told my mother about it often so that she would not worry, and she believed I was safe in the trench whenever an air raid siren rang out.

At the foot of the cedar hill was a gas tank which fueled the kitchens of Nagasaki and at the top of the hill was a wooden hut of about four and one-half tatami mat size. The girl students whispered that the army stored its ammunition there. Occasionally, a uniformed soldier went up among the cedar trees to the arsenal. I didn't tell my mother about those two things, or the fact that it took at least ten minutes for us to run from our work area to the trench.

Early the next morning, on the 10th, it was still dark outside when my mother was awakened by knocking at the back door. "Sae-san, Sae-san," a man's voice called. It was Takano, a reporter from the West Japan Press. "Nagasaki is wiped out," Takano shouted from the back gate, as my mother looked out from the hallway, sliding open one of the rain doors. "The high school students at the plant, too, are all gone." With that, he ran toward the mis-blanketed river, making a loud noise with his shoes.

Takano's news did not register with my mother for a while. Only when she realized that the wholesale destruction of Nagasaki included her daughter's death, did she fall to her knees in the corridor. My aunt and uncle, who had also heard, hurried in from the back gate. "The medical school seems to be on fire, Sae-san," my aunt said. "Nobody says they are dead," my uncle scolded her. He wore a khaki civilian uniform and an iron hat, and a megaphone hung from his shoulder, ready for emergency. My mother said trembling, "I hear the munitions plant is destroyed, too, brother."

"They wouldn't have killed schoolgirls," he pleaded, a meaningless consolation.

With the bombing of August 9th, communication with Nagasaki ceased. No trains could get through either. Some seemed to go only as far as Nagayo or Michi-no-O, completely off schedule. On the evening of the 9th, according to the Hiroshima-Nagasaki Atomic Bomb Exhibit, the Isahaya Navy Hospital rescue team of fifty, the Omura navy rescue team of three, and ten members of the Isahaya Medical Group left for Nagasaki to provide first-aid. Hindered by fire from entering Nagasaki, the rescue team spent the night just outside the city tending the wounded who had been carried there. The number of rescue personnel from the suburbs was much too small.

Right after the bombing I spotted a doctor at work. He was examining patients all by himself, seated on a small cooking stove from someone's burnt-out house. All he had for medication was an alum pot full of mercurochrome. Bomb victims filed up, but they were all lightly wounded. The badly wounded rolled on the ground, unable to get up. The doctor himself had a wound on the head which dripped blood from beneath a towel wrapped around it. I wondered about his family. He seemed to be a doctor who practiced at home, but no house nearby had survived—his family must have perished or been very seriously wounded. I admired him, but I feel sad to think that even then, in the mind-shattering disaster of the atomic bomb, people could not break out of their occupational frames: doctors from their medical duties and soldiers from their military consciousness. A soldier ran past, holding up a dismembered arm, saying that he had to report to headquarters: he had no time to stop for medical care. Some flung off everything but their personal values; others remained thoroughly faithful to society. The war proved to be a subtle director of the human drama.

Following the navy and medical rescue teams, youth groups from Aino and Chijiwa went by truck to join the relief work. They had been instructed to bring a towel each to use for a mask, since the job was digging out bodies. Inatomi was among them. He was a student at the medical school, but had stayed home with a cold that day and escaped the bombing. He had gone to Aino Station on the Shimabara Railway, but, not feeling up to fighting the morning rush, had gone back home. He was in the same year as my cousin and we knew each other.

Loaded with shovels, spades, modest supplies of medication, riceballs and water, the youth group's truck went from Isahaya to Kigitsu, swung toward Yagami, and entered the city through Karls' Springs on the opposite side of Urakami, passing N Girls' High School. The Nishiyama area was not burning when Inatomi and the others entered Urakami early on the morning of the 10th.

On August 9th, I went to the factory in dark slacks and a short-sleeved blouse, with wooden clogs on my bare feet. My older sister had made the slacks out of thick Chinese satinette that my father sent us from overseas. I wore nothing under my white broadcloth blouse with its tailored collar; for underwear I had on white bloomers with an elastic band at the waist. I had a watch on my left wrist. It was a German watch with a band of silver links, also sent by my father. The only definite burn I had from the bomb was under my watchband. When I took off the watch, I noticed for the first time that a blister had formed within the circle of each link. The three- to four-millimeter round blisters made a chain around my wrist. I felt uncomfortable until they healed, but they went away without becoming infected, unlike the red spots on my arms and legs which were infected for a month.

My hair was long, down to my waist. I braided it, because loose hair could get caught in the machine. It was dangerous, for if a lot of hair got caught and the machine were not stopped immediately, the whole head would be caught, for hair will not tear away from the scalp. A student with long, loose hair had died that way. Braid long hair; if not long enough to braid, bind it with a rubberband: that was a strict rule at the factory. If I had not braided my hair, the wind caused by the bomb explosion would have blown it up like the hands of the thousand-armed Kannon, and it would have caught in the debris of the demolished building and delayed my escape.

My work place, Section A of the Engineering Department, was a wooden building and it caught fire several minutes after the explosion. Section A recycled scrap iron, waste paper and coal from in the factory. The workers there too, seemed to have been cycled away from the normal route: a somewhat retarded woman, a man with a limp, the assistant chief who had lost an arm, and a middle-aged man who was always grinning; otherwise they were perfectly healthy, but only the foreman was in excellent physical condition, his body intact. I wondered why he had not been drafted, since he was still in his early forties. They seemed to transfer to Section A workers wounded elsewhere within the same factory. Perhaps it was out of thoughtfulness, and yet to me it was cruel to shove the maimed into obscure corners to tend the factory trash.

A few days after we joined Section A, I was trapped in the waste paper recycling hut by the worker with one short leg and the middle-aged grinning man. One of them entered the hut, and with his arms raised, cornered me at the other end of the room. The somewhat retarded woman watched from behind the man at the entrance, giggling. Just then, the foreman caught on, and he yelled at them. He held me standing scared in the corner, but even as he assured me, "Don't worry," he was stroking me between the thighs. Incredible as it may seem, that was the way things were in the work mobilization program. Morals were extremely corrupt in factories then, and the notion of the "divine empire" was remote.

Three girls were sent to Section A from N Girls' High School—Yoko, Akiko, and myself. Before allocating the students, the factory gave us a physical examination. Since work areas producing machinery involved heavy work in dirty air, they wanted no weak students there, and three of us were not chosen. After such extra tests as blood precipitation, temperature, and X-rays, they decided we could handle no more than the easygoing work of Section A, where no one did hard labor. I guess we were unwanted people.

Section A was a wooden building, actually a shed. Our work was recycling, and of course the building, too, was made of recycled materials. The windows were fashioned from odd pieces of wood and a medley of glass, triangular-colored pieces mixed with clear glass cut to fit. There was even a stained glass piece occupying the corner of one window.

When there was no job, I used to look at the windows and imagine what they had been before recycling. My friends called it the beggar's hut.

Our fragile "beggar's hut" turned out to have advantages at the time of the bombing. Three friends who worked in the heavy, three-storey red brick building burned to death under the bricks. Friends who worked in the Engineering Department, of which our section was a branch, became porcupines, filled with glass needles from the shattering of the huge windows that illuminated the work of drawing. After thirty years, glass splinters remain in their bodies and from time to time, they move. When the glass presses into the flesh, the pain is unbearable. An X-ray is taken to prepare for an operation, but by then, the splinter is no longer where it was. The doctor once quipped to a friend of mine, "This is your medal. Leave it in your body." It is easy to treat things lightly when one is not the victim.

The atomic bomb carrier glided into the Nagasaki sky without engine noise. It was 10:58. We girls were in the office of Section A along with the foreman, the one-armed assistant chief, and Yamaguchi, a member of the female volunteer corps of Kagoshima, six altogether. The windows of stained and colored glass were open toward Urakami. Three chimneys stood ten meters from the windows. They were twenty meters tall and as wide as two tatami mats. We looked out on the concrete court where high school boys were dancing in a circle, a dance of farewell to send off a friend to the front. In those days, young students left every day, and the bleak concrete court of the factory had become the place of their ritual.

I was sitting at the desk with the windows and the chimneys on my left. In front of me was the foreman. He had no shirt on and his robust bare chest was dripping with sweat. Akiko sat close to the window and Yoko with her back to it. The one-armed assistant chief sat close by on the foreman's left. This man always hovered around the boss, obsequious and flattering. Just then he was fanning the sweaty foreman with a notebook. Yamaguchi stood on my left, one hand on the window side of my desk.

There was still time before lunch but we were a random group with nothing to talk about. "Feel better?" asked the one-armed assistant chief, fanning away. I think the foreman was eating something. "Yeah," he grunted, swallowing. That ended the conversation, and the room was quiet. The figures danced on in the court, a pantomime in broad daylight. Then the sound of an engine approached from Michi-no-O. Yamaguchi turned toward the foreman, and asked, "Isn't that an airplane?" The foreman listened. "Sounds like an airplane," he said, "Take a look." Yamaguchi leaned out the stained glass window, but returned. "Nothing's there."

"There's been no siren. It couldn't be an enemy plane," said the assistant chief. The sound stopped. It happened in a fraction of a second.

Suddenly, like the sound of a huge plane sharply dropping or rising, a

great blast tore the sky asunder. "Air raid!" a woman cried. Then there
was not another sound. I saw no flash of light and heard no explosion,
though the bomb was nicknamed *pika-don*, flash-and-boom. Nor did I
feel the 360 meter-per-second wind. The next thing I knew I was under
a shattered building.

People near the target area hardly heard the explosion, but they
heard a great whirring when the airplane suddenly rose. After it dropped
the atomic bomb, the B-29 quickly ascended. Of course, *they* had no in-
tention of dying. Kill the engine, drop the bomb, swerve up and get out
fast—they must have practiced that over and over again.

Between the sound of the accelerating engines of the swerving plane
and the demolition of the factory, there was a split-second to shout one
word, "air raid." In that breath of time, 73,889 people died instantly.
Approximately the same number, 74,909, were hurled out in the blazing
summer sun, stripped of their skin, like the legendary white rabbit of Inaba who was flayed alive by the crocodile.

Right after the bombing, I found myself blinded. Though my eyes
were open, I saw nothing. There was only darkness. Darkness that has
depth gives me no fear because I can look into it and still be sure of my
sight. But now a flat darkness tightly covered my eyes. I'm blinded, I
thought. Yoko and Akiko also said later that they thought they had
been blinded, and rubbed their eyes with both hands. Those who were
looking directly at the flash of the bomb did lose their sight. The fire
ball of the atomic bomb was seventy meters in diameter. Rumor has it
that an already blind person recovered his sight from the flash, but I
think that is fiction. Yet the atomic flash was so incredibly awesome as
to permit any fantasy.

I think I was hurled down by the wind of the explosion. I found myself crouched under a desk, able to move somewhat. But when I tried to
change position, although nothing was pressing hard on me, pieces of
wood caught at my body. Not understanding why I was in this condition, I remained still for a while, crouching under the demolished building. Once given the habit of thinking, one first tries to understand before taking action. The animal instinct that remains in man works for a
brief moment only; after that, analysis takes over. The moment we realize we are alive, the subconscious instinct has been overridden.

The darkness faded into a pale light that grew into the color of hy-
drangea just beginning to bloom. There was neither heat nor coolness. It
was the light of death stuck there, like a wall. This was what was later
identified as the flash from the 300,000 degree centigrade explosion.
Logically, I must have seen the flash, and was so dazzled by it that I saw
only darkness.

I tried to raise a piece of wood my hand happened to touch, to see if
it moved. I pushed at it twice, but it did not move. I tried over and over
to shove it away, but the wood stayed firm. Suddenly I was frightened.

Near the waste paper recycling area of Section A, I could see flames. Smoke started to stream my way.

I would be burnt to death if I didn't run away, I thought. Forcing myself to be calm, I looked at the pillars and piled-up jumble of boards around me and I saw a plank above my head, which looked like the top of a desk. There was a slit in it. If I pushed it forward, maybe it would slide. I thrust my hands into the slit, and pushed hard. The board slid back easily and revealed a small patch of sky. There was barely room for me to slip out.

When I stood up, the split timber tore the left shoulder of my blouse and scratched the skin. The whole area was covered with ashes, and things were catching fire everywhere. Black smoke, red smoke, curled up and avalanched, whirring into the bare court. The one-armed assistant chief came running out in front of me. Holding his arm up in the air, he ran shouting into the court. The foreman ran after him, protecting his crewcut head with his hands, his back hunched over. He had a wound in the back. "Foreman!" I called, but intent on his own escape, he ran on into the flaming court.

The shortest way to the main gate of the munitions plant was across the court. The plant was tightly guarded because of the nature of the production—secret arms. The outside walls were made of reinforced concrete, and the rear entrance beside Section A was an iron door, usually bolted with an iron lock. You could get in only through the main gate and a few small employee entrances. To get out of the plant, there was no other way but to follow the director.

Section A was now almost completely ablaze, and flames streamed and roared into the court from all over the plant. It was impossible to get across the court. Peering through the smoke, I saw a boy in a tank shirt running toward the back of Section A, toward the concrete wall and iron door. I knew the wall was too high to climb, and there was no foothold, but the boy kept on going, so instantly I followed. Then I found the wall shattered, revealing iron bars. Through the gaping hole I saw the field outside the factory. I gasped. It was not just the munitions plant that had been hit. I had thought safety lay outside the factory if I could escape, but now I realized that the field was even more badly damaged. Inside the factory, the smoke that partially hid the area had saved me from despair, but now I was stunned.

Many of those who were outdoors are said to have died from the pressure of the explosion. Most of the students dancing in the court were killed instantly; the others suffered from burns and lived about two hours. One student was hurled against the concrete wall by the pressure, and his body was crushed, exposing his internal organs. Being young, he groaned loudly. A friend who heard him while running away even now covers her ears when talking about him. There were at least forty in the dancing circle, including some college students.

It is a sad dance, a silent ceremony of students sending a friend to the front. The student who is leaving stands in the middle, his fellow students making a circle around him, arms linked. The leader calls out and the circle swings to the right, everyone lifting their left foot. They hop with the right foot to the rhythm, then put down the left. Alternating feet, the circle turns to the right, little by little. From time to time, the leader calls out. As they move to the right, the students' wooden clogs make a rasping sound on the concrete. The echoless noise sounded vacant to me, like a wave that surged up but did not run back. I had come across such a circle many times. I could not just pass by; I would stop and nod silently to the student in the middle. When our eyes met, he would return the bow—a boy with a white band across his shoulder symbolizing loyalty unto death.

The students give a cheer after the silent dance is done. The leader calls out the name of a girls' school and those in the circle interested in it clap their hands. The leader looks at the student in the center. If he only taps his forefingers together, he means "My girl goes to another school." The leader tries more nearby schools, sometimes even outside Nagasaki prefecture, until the student responds with loud clapping. All the students in the circle cheer loudly, and again they dance shoulder to shoulder. It is the same dance as before, but this time they sing too, the anthem of the boy's high school. The tempo gradually rises until the dance is a frenzy. Then it halts.

Thank you—the departing students bows.

Let's meet again—the rest return the bow. It is a simple farewell, a ritual of mourning. The last group that I saw all died, one in the center and the others around him. I remember a meeting with a student who was later killed in the battle of Okinawa. Maiguma was the undisputed slob among the students at Kumamoto Higher School. He was enjoying the sun in the court. The all-clear had sounded and I was pattering across it when he called, "Hey!" and beckoned me over. When I approached, he held open a seam in his uniform and chuckled "Let's play hunt the lice. It's fun when they run away." Then, he warned me in a whisper not to tell anyone and parodied a solemn reading of the opening line of the Imperial Rescript on Education: Know ye, Our Subjects, "We broke wind involuntarily, you our subjects must find it malodorous. Pray withstand it for a second." At first I didn't get it. When I understood the meaning the second time around, I burst out laughing and said, "No, no! Not God incarnate!"

"The military police will kill you if you laugh. Keep looking serious even if it's funny," he said. In those days, I had no worries.

The ones I saw escape from Section A were the foreman, assistant chief, and the middle-aged man who was always grinning. Yamaguchi died instantly. A beam dropped, reportedly, on her collarbone, and crushed her shoulders and chin. She died clamped between a desk and the beam before the flames reached Section A. Instant death is best if it is an atomic bomb. A worker who lived a day or two after the bombing tore off his own flesh out of suffering.

Akiko and Yoko were safe. They had burns, but not serious ones, and could help each other escape the flames engulfing Section A. I had made my escape before them. "You ran so fast! We thought you had gone crazy," they say now laughing. To me their smiling eyes seemed a thin-veiled reproof for my cowardice. Since I cannot laugh with them, I try not to see them often. Akiko's family all died. Her parents died instantly at home in Take-no-Kubo, and her older brother at Nagasaki Medical School where he was a student. After the war, all of Akiko's hair fell out. Her features were somewhat Western, with deep-set eyes and clear-cut features. When she went bald, her eyes grew even bigger than before, and she reminded me of a French doll thrown into a toybox after its hair is all torn out.

Two years ago I happened to learn that she lives in the same seaside town as I do now, and so telephoned her. She told me she was going to the hospital in a few days for a stomach operation, to add to the scars and patches all over her body from previous operations. One of them was twenty years ago, for breast cancer. This time they would not know if she had cancer until they opened her stomach.

"It's cancer. I know it when I press it with my fingers. I feel stiff from the breast to the shoulder, too. It was just like this when I had breast cancer. I am pretty sure."

"What are you doing now?" I changed the topic.

"I have just finished the curtains in the children's room." She stopped short. She said she had to be doing something; otherwise she would be frightened. Since then, two years have passed, and I have hesitated to call.

My mother died...

My wife is dead...

My daughter-in-law passed away... I cannot face those answers when I call.

I was virtually unharmed. While freeing myself from the rubble of the wooden building I scratched my shoulder and knees. Glass fragments were stuck in the back of my head in the part of my hair. Running to the mountains, I could feel them and pulled out two slivers. The blood stained my fingertips, but did not flow.

Those in dark clothing, it is said, had bad burns because of its absorption of the heat. Perhaps I escaped that danger because I was wearing a white blouse. Could it be that the three tall chimneys protected me, or that Yamaguchi, who met instant death, absorbed all the light, keeping the others safe? Life and death pull at each other till they stand back to back, in a balance more delicate than tissue paper.

The *Asahi* of October 10, 1970, carried an article under the headline: "Monster Cartoons of Atomic Bomb Patients in Shogakkan's *Second*

Grader's Monthly: Middle School Student Criticizes Cruelty of Cartoons."
A middle school girl was reported to have declared that it was cruel to
liken an atomic bomb patient to a monster. Her controversial comment
referred to "Super Planetman," one of forty-five monsters illustrated in
the special monster issue of the magazine. This monster, also called
"Atomic Bomb Planetman," has a human shape but is covered with kel-
oid scars. Questioned about his intentions, the publisher said he could
not comment until he investigated the matter. Members of the group
known as Readers of Atomic Bomb Documents, strongly attacked the
illustration.

The incident really did leave a deep impression on us. It was a taste
of the cruelty of Time-equals-Oblivion. But the atomic bomb needs no
sentimentality. Let them be, the cartoonists. Whether they draw monsters or clowns, they will stimulate someone to feel something about the
bombing. Now, thirty years later, it has become difficult to portray the
facts as they were.

Akiko suffered from cancer of the breast at age twenty. According to
the survey (1956-67) of malignant tumors in in-patients at the Hiroshima
Atomic Bomb Hospital, breast cancer ranks third after stomach and lung
cancer. Since the latter are found in both sexes, the rate of breast cancer
is quite high. To sixty cases of lung cancer, there are fifty-one of breast
cancer. Recently, however, it has become more difficult to obtain the
medical treatment and benefits provided to bomb victims, because certi-
fication is harder to get. An atomic bomb victim certificate is issued on
approval by the minister of public welfare and more than twenty members of the Medical Council on Atomic Bomb Victims. Akiko should
naturally be a certified bomb victim, but fatigue overcame her in the
middle of the cumbersome procedures. It is hard for a sick person to
move. Even if she could, the endless red tape would simply exhaust her
as was the case with me when I applied for a Special Handbook.

Most ridiculous is that the application has to be endorsed with the
seals of three people who can testify that the person was there at the
time of the bombing. Three witnesses means three workers in the same
work area or classmates sent to the same factory. It is next to impossible
to find as many as three living witnesses. I wonder if that rule is less
strict now. The certificate helps a patient financially by promising free
medication, so there might be a temptation to cheat, yet really, there is
no need to require three witnesses. The title of atomic bomb victim is
no honor. Since it involves problems of genes, one would rather conceal
such a record. The painfulness of life for people like Akiko and myself is
year by year narrowing down to a problem that touches only ourselves.

Cartoon or otherwise, anything that conveys the pain of the victims
of the bombing is acceptable to me. The disastrous scene that I glimpsed
through the gaping hole in the wall of Section A offered a host of cartoon monsters. The victims stood on the field, drapes of flesh hanging
from all over their bodies.

Outside the wall was the road to Michi-no-O and across the road was a grass field. The Urakami River ran along the field, with a narrow trail perpendicular to the river going into the range of mountains including Mt. Konpira. Half of the city of Nagasaki was sheltered from the atomic bomb by this mountain.

From late July through early August 1945, the number of air raids had increased. The airplanes did not attack, but just flew over, causing repeated warning and air raid sirens. At each siren students were supposed to retreat to the trenches in a designated mountain area, while regular workers remained on the job. The one-armed assistant chief complained. "All you students do is run away. Who is left to die?" It was a legitimate question. There was no reason why only the lives of students should have been specially protected. So we balked and even though we were supposed to run at each air raid siren, we responded only every other time. Three teachers, Miss T., Miss M., and Miss K. from N Girls' High School had been transferred to our factory as proctors. When we asked about the ruling on shelter, oval-faced Miss K. said, "You have been mobilized to work in the factory, but you remain students of N High School. You must obey your teachers about when to run. But the trench is too far and it is dangerous. Let's think of another place." She negotiated with the factory and obtained permission for us to take refuge in a trench they had just started to dig in the field.

This new bomb shelter was to be sturdy, reinforced with concrete. It was being dug by members of a volunteer girls corps. They were young girls of twelve or thirteen, just out of higher elementary school.

We could hear their merry voices from the field in the morning. Perhaps fat and pale shiny earthworms jumped on the shovel that scooped the dirt and there would be a lively girlish scream. Taking a moment from her work, Yoko went to watch them through a narrow slit in the iron door. She returned saying, "They're as jolly as if they were on a school outing."

The field was a flat green covered with dandelions, wild violets, and blue purslanes. Alongside the diggers, young children from the neighborhood were plucking flowers, escorted by an old woman. They spread a little white cotton handkerchief on the grass, and placed their flowers on it. The addition of a dandelion made the pale wild flowers beam with glee.

While the little children played on the grass, the old woman with some others collected waste coal from the street. Every morning Section A workers threw the waste coal from the factory out into the street, partly to mend the dirt road. Neighborhood housewives scavenged the better pieces from the waste. They used only a small amount at home because of its strong heat and sold the rest for pocket money. I had become friends with the old woman and little girls. At lunchtime, I used to go all the way around through the main gate to the field to help them gather flowers and coal.

The field disappeared in the split-second of the flash. One of the children had been a light-complexioned, short-haired little girl. Her grandmother was petite and, like the girl, fair skinned. Now she sat in the burning field clutching the child. Half of the girl's scalp had been ripped open, and her short straight hair hung from her cheek. She lay dead with her lips and eyes open. Childlike loveliness remained only around her mouth, where her white front teeth showed. The old woman's flesh was flaked and tattered like a mop. The girls of the volunteers corps also stood torn, like mops. The oozing grease of their flesh shone like the skin of reptiles. Trembling, they were saying to each other, "doesn't this hurt, doesn't this hurt?" They were weeping, their headbands still declaring, "Sacrifice self to serve the country!" The directors of the drama of war often create harlequins.

What kind of bomb was it that could cause this kind of disaster in a second, we wondered. "I hear they dropped a lot of big cans of kerosene and then scattered incendiary shells over them," said a man who seemed to be a factory worker.

"They must have, because there is fire everywhere. There's no other way to explain it. I'll bet this burn came from touching kerosene without knowing it." The woman looked at the burn on her arm.

"So that clanging was from the oil cans," said a woman holding the hand of a five- or six-year-old boy.

Those who could talk while running up the mountain trail were only lightly wounded. Among the badly wounded, those who were walking were well off. There were many who collapsed in the path or lay on the slope, unable to move. They had different kinds of burns. In some cases white fat showed where the surface of the skin was burnt away. Some burns were red, filled with blood, making more white rabbits of Inaba.

A Nagasaki University Medical School atomic bomb first-aid report, "Explosion Pressure and Skin Tearing," appeared in the *Asahi Weekly*. It explained,

> It was originally thought that the skin peeled as a result of the vacuum pressure formed at the time of the explosion of the bomb, or that it came off with pieces of clothing blown off by the great pressure. We realized later that if our first theory were correct, the skin should have been torn off all over the body. Actually, that occurred only in areas exposed to the light. Probably the two causes should be considered together: first heat rays caused burns on the skin, seriously weakening it, and that was quickly followed by powerful pressure acting on the skin. The healthy portions remained on the body, but the burnt parts were torn off. Thus, it seems that the tearing of the skin is the result of both burns and pressure.

"Tearing of the skin" is an apt description, for it conveys the pain of forcing skin away from flesh.

Some people had neither open wounds nor cuts but were swollen all over. As a result of receiving heat rays evenly over the entire body, they were covered with watery blisters. The eyes and nose and lips were warped with opaque white water under one piece of thin skin. A fish baked in a microwave oven comes out white without burns. This type of burn resembled the baked fish. Areas with blisters had swollen to double the normal size.

Another type of burn caused frills of skin to dangle from both arms, like the thin peel of newly harvested young potatoes. A middle school student with tattered arms climbed up Mt. Konpira crying to himself, "It hurts, oh, it hurts!"

The Children of God conducted all kinds of experiments on burns and human bodies, it seems.

After the war students from the universities of Kyushu and Nagasaki came to N Girls' High School to do a survey. They inquired about the girls' health before the bombing and the effects afterwards. They also asked about changes in menstruation after the bombing. Some students refused to cooperate. "There is no need to supply material concerning the atomic bomb anymore," they said.

The atomic bomb left wounds on the body and in the mind. A dying man asked for medicine. His death was evident to everyone. There was no way of helping him, but still he asked in a low voice, "Please, some medicine." It must have been hell in his mind.

"We're getting a doctor, so you must stay strong," I tried to cheer him up.

"That's what you say ... but he doesn't come," he said. "But he doesn't come" ... these words still echo in my heart, and I taste a lingering bitterness in them.

One or two hours after the bomb I went to Matsuyama-machi, the center of the attack. I would not have been so foolhardy had I known the terror of radiation. I met two uninjured women in the mountains. They were the only ones I'd seen whose clothes were not torn, and I wanted to stay with them. On no other occasion have healthy people looked so rare and delightful as then. They were on their way home from Michi-no-O where they had planned to buy flour. Michi-no-O was 3.5 kilometers from the epicenter. They had been unable to buy flour; and instead carried sprouting seed potatoes in their bags.

They had started early in the morning to get back by noon. Not waiting for the train, they had headed for home on foot across the mountains. They saw the flash in the mountains. "It's near," they had said to each other, and since the potatoes were lunch for their families, hurried on their way. As they approached Urakami, they noticed an odor, and then they saw wounded people beginning to approach, one after another. The two women stopped one who could talk and asked what was happening. Without stopping, he said simply, "I don't know how we got this way."

They decided to go home anyway. The trail led them to the hill at the back of the munitions plant. This is where I met them. They told me they lived in Matsuyama-machi. One in *kasuri*-patterned *mompe* trousers said, "First we have to go to Matsuyama-machi to see how our families are. If everything is all right then I will walk you home," and asked me where I lived. "I live in Junin-machi." They started off in good spirits, believing Matsuyama-machi to be safe, since the attack had centered on the munitions plant. I no longer had my clogs. I had been walking barefooted on the mountain trail without noticing it.

We stood in the rice paddies on the slope of the hills at the back of Matsuyama-machi. The town had disappeared. The woman in *kasuri* trousers gazed mute on the ruined town that had turned brown. The other woman in black trousers caught up with us from behind. Her body seemed to fold over as she shrieked in a voice wrung out from her insides, "My house... it's gone!"

Then she started to cry, repeating, "Grandma died, Grandma died..."

Matsuyama-machi was a plain, as though tilled with spades. Before, it had small, low houses, with electric poles and small factories standing out. Many houses subcontracted work for the munitions plant or the iron foundry, or mended pots and pans. It was a town where the smell of broiling sardines floated in shady alleys, where families lived humbly together. I liked the feeling of the town and often got off the train there on my way home from work and wandered around. Sometimes I met Inatomi there to enjoy the hours after work. An old man had sat on the dirt floor in the shadows, blowing his bellows. The fire glowed and flared, lighting up his good-natured face. Inatomi went in and lightly asked what he was making. It had been a town which enjoyed a modest happiness. Now those houses were all gone, and the people who lived in them were gone, too.

Some of the seriously wounded with bad burns lay on the terraced fields, but they did not come to even ten percent of Matsuyama-machi's population. The woman in black slacks kept crying out, "Grandma, Grandma." They had been a family of mother and daughter. "Don't cry," the woman in *kasuri* trousers shouted, "If it has come to this, the only choice is vengeance; it's no time for weeping."

Vengeance—the word weighed deep in my mind. Face to face with this disastrous sight, I felt sad to see the strength of the heart ready to turn mourning into desperate revenge. It was horrifying even to imagine adding more unsightly people—handless, legless, eyeless. Nagasaki prefecture would become filled with such people. Man is happiest when he has both hands, both legs, and two eyes and a nose.

The death rate within 0.5 kilometers of the target of the bombing was 98.4 percent. Of this number, the percentage who died immediately or on the same day was 90.4. Those who lay on the pumpkin terraces probably died that day also. Four hundred meters away from the epicenter, roof tiles melted and flowed away. Concrete roads melted and became filled with bubbles. Pebbles on the roadside also melted. It was the heat of lava flowing from a crater. Human beings, with their tender bones and flesh, were more fragile than ephemera thrown into a gas fire.

When I read the results and statistics on the bombing, I don't understand why such a shattering weapon was necessary to kill men. On the other hand, life's toughness is also surprising. In September, the month after the bombing, foxtails and other weeds sprouted on the burnt-out fields. The life that had remained in the earth began to stir right after the bombing. It was reported, however, that the influence of radiation caused abnormal cell division. Plants were short of chlorophyll, hence there were white spots on the leaves, and some leaves were deformed and wrinkled. Other instances of natural disturbance frequently reported around that time in Nagasaki included twin eggplants, twin pumpkins, and abnormal clusters of fruit on a tomato plant.

A friend of mine, Ikeuchi, lost all her straight, black hair, and later curly red hair grew in. It was red like Maureen O'Hara's and had beautiful waves. She laughed, saying that her new curly locks had grown in because it had been Americans who dropped the bomb.

I will never forget how moved I was when I found weeds on the bombed area. On the way to school, in the crack of the concrete platform at Urakami Station, I saw a single stalk of grass. It had white flowers like sesame seeds. This was in a place where it was said no grass would grow for sixty years to come. The life of a weed seemed to promise life to us, too. I, too, can live, I thought, the tears welling up.

I don't remember exactly when, but roughly two hours after the bomb I started to feel nauseous. I vomited in the middle of the field. All I brought up was white foam. The woman in *kasuri* trousers with whom I was walking picked a pumpkin from the field, saying, "It's because you haven't eaten lunch." The leaves and stem were all burnt or blown away, but the fruit of the pumpkin remained. She broke it with a jagged piece of slate and handed me some, telling me to eat. The smell made me vomit again. The woman said, "Your tummy is empty. That's why you are throwing up. Even if you don't want to, you've got to eat something." When I still hesitated, she admonished me, "We don't know how many days we will be in this situation, so you must eat."

The pumpkin had been rolling in the sun-scorched field and it was warm and pungent. Trying to crush it between my teeth, I vomited again at the raw smell. It was a thick smell like ripe summer grass. When human skin dries in the sun, it smells the same. Somebody said that a tomato has the smell of blood. I think the same about pumpkins.

"The sun's falling! shouted an old man in a cotton padded air raid hat, pointing toward the sun. It had turned a vermillion red and was falling in an eddying motion, clearly shimmering like the sun in a Van Gogh painting. That midsummer sun at midday which we saw from the terrace field was at eye level. The sun's heat lets one feel the grace of life even in

the hottest summer, but just then, it was cruel. It was as hot as though it
had been rolled flat and covered the earth. The woman quickly opened
the umbrella that she carried for a parasol and hid the sun from view.
"Don't look at something that scares you." Even under the umbrella my
cheeks and arms were burning painfully.

"I'm sure Isahaya is all right, but if it was bombed, come to my home.
I am all alone now, too..."

The woman in *kasuri* trousers wrote down on a piece of paper the address of her family home in Shimabara, and she took a ten-yen note from
her purse. "This is just enough to cover the traveling expenses to Shimabara, so don't lose it." She folded the bill small and pushed it between
the straps of my slacks.

"When you are alone, you need money, so don't drop it," she said
again.

The atomic bomb first aid report stated:

> Though it was made public that a new type of bomb had been
> dropped on Hiroshima, no details were known and countermeas-
> ures for citizens were not reinforced. Consequently, when on Aug-
> ust 9, Nagasaki was attacked with the same bomb, the military,
> the government, and citizens were all totally unprepared, even
> those of us who had an interest in atomic bombs, we were sorry to
> admit, did not realize until we were informed by the leaflets scat-
> tered by the enemy that night that it was an atomic bomb.

If it was so with specialists, then could we be blamed for naively imagining that the enemy had dropped a large quantity of kerosene tanks
and then showered incendiary bombs to ignite them? Had we known
that an atomic bomb had been dropped, we would not have eaten pumpkins in the field at Matsuyama-machi. At this writing what strikes me as
odd is the sweet potatoes that those women had bought at Michi-no-O.
Instead of eating pumpkin a la radioactivity, we could have eaten those
sweet potatoes. When we sat in the field, the woman in *kasuri* trousers
held them on her lap. Like everybody else, she also was confused.

But my nausea was not because of hunger. It was a disease caused by
radioactivity, called radioactive hangover. The atomic bomb prepared a
way toward death even for those who had no external wounds. The
younger the body was, the greater the disturbance. Children exposed to
radioactivity near the target area almost all died within three days. They
died of proleptic disturbances in the digestive organs.

From August 9 on, Isahaya city housed the sick and wounded in the
Navy Hospital, city schools, and all other public places. Green bottle
flies swarmed, attracted by the smell of the wounds. They rested on human bodies and maggots hatched and fed on them. Things that damaged
what vestiges remained of "human dignity" occurred before our eyes.
War teaches man the providence of nature. We learned that damp wood
was best for burning human bodies. It does not catch fire quickly, but

once it does, it gives more powerful heat than thoroughly dried wood.
And since it sustains fire, the body burns well, instead of just halfway.
Then flesh becomes indistinguishable from wood. It is slightly darker,
but when raked into the earth, the ashes assimilate completely.

In the fire the internal organs burst with a sound. The grease splashed
and flared as sparks ignited it in the air. The sudden spread of the flames
in the wide darkness was beautiful, and as unexpected as the appearance
of a picture drawn with invisible ink. I was carried away by its beauty,
and would almost anticipate the brilliant moment, thinking, 'Now it will
flare up.'

Recently, I read a report about the survivors of an airplane accident
in the Andes. They were left for seventy days in the snow of the mountains, but sixteen miraculously returned alive. They were young people
all around thirty, devout Christians, intellectuals, and upper class. The
event became headline news because they had survived by eating human
flesh. First they refused to feed on the flesh of the dead. Some of the survivors, however, persuaded the others saying that the fellow passengers
who had died were given by God as provision for the rest to live. So they
had eaten. In a few days, everybody was eating human flesh. By the end
they had even searched out the bodies of those survivors who had died
in an avalanche a few days after the crash, because they proved to have
higher nutritional value. When discovered by the rescue team, some of
them had made the skulls of their friends into dishes to enhance the
pleasure of their meal. They had also made spoons out of bones. The report vividly portrays the horrible reality of how the principles of these
well-educated people could be gradually eroded, their adjustment to cannibalism growing so complete that the moralism of the highflown phrase
"the dignity of Man" seems altogether irrelevant.

If it is God's will, whether it be atomic bombs showered "in fury" or
eating human flesh given "as provision for the living," such trespasses
would not really impair human dignity. What hurts, however, is that the
flow of time—Oblivion—washes away the details of an extreme situation,
while only the most sensational parts are remembered.

It was so with the woman in *kasuri* trousers. We stayed nearly an
hour on the terraced field of Matsuyama-machi, but she and her friend
did not look for their families. The ruins of Matsuyama-machi showed
complete destruction allowing no shadow of hope. Yet wonder of won-
ders, the husband of the woman in *kasuri* trousers had survived. He
worked at a factory in Aku-no-Ura, which faces Nagasaki across the bay.
The place suffered only small losses from the bombing; if he had gone to
work that day, he would naturally have been safe. However, like Inatomi,
he had stayed home with a cold. He had felt uncomfortable because
warning sirens had been sounding from morning, so he carried his mat-
tress into the shelter dug in the dirt floor of their house. The two-storey
wooden house was blown into a thousand pieces. The only remainder

was a water tank, made of artificial granite, and out from under crawled
the man. The mouth of the trench had been completely blocked, so it
took him three hours to shovel his way out. He burned the sole of his
foot while running away but that was his only external wound.

At the end of October, after the war, when I went with my mother to
Shimabara to say thanks, the man, completely bald, lay in the main room.
It was a farm house looking down on the Sea of Chijiwa. I could clearly
see the color of the sea change with huge schools of fish.

As my mother thanked them for helping her daughter, the man lifted
his body and said, "When I was desperately digging in the trench like a
mole, this person was just looking down from the field. She didn't even
come to help." The lips of the woman moved as she served tea, but she
stared at the sea, saying nothing. Any instance we might choose to dis-
cuss reveals many such ironies.

From Matsuyama-machi, we moved into the shelter of the mountains
again, avoiding the city as we headed home. We arrived at the hill at the
back of N Girls' High School in the late afternoon. It is near the area called the Seven-Faced Great Bodhisattva Mountain. The one or two farm-
houses there were half destroyed by the wind from the bombing. A
chicken stretched its neck and peeped from a pile of broken beams as we
passed by. "What happened?" it seemed to ask. This made us smile.
'Even humans don't understand,' I wanted to say, as if the chicken could
understand.

Nagasaki sits in a basin. The evening sun lingered there coloring it red.
The concrete building of Sako Primary School stood on the lefthand
side as we faced the business section. On the red clay of the schoolyard
there were several children. A moist wind blew comfortably through the
undamaged town. I felt the warmth of a town where families survived.

When I first saw the burnt out site of Matsuyama-machi, I thought of
the old man blowing his bellows. I thought of a happy family around the
fire broiling sardines. Again, looking down at the town in the breeze, I
thought of families: the nest of a family surrounded by logs and tiles; an
ordinary house with a dirt floor, screen doors discolored by the sun, and
lighted by dim electric bulbs; the ordinary family who lived there. As far
as I am concerned, neither destruction nor peace relates to anything but
families; the nation is always a remote entity. As we shifted our gaze
from Sako Primary School, Kaisei Middle School stood out on a nearby
hill. Its elegant building, once light gray but now painted in camouflage
colors, was undamaged.

Junin-machi, where I lodged, was a town right below that middle
school. The row of houses there still stood intermingled with stone fences and yellow rose bushes. Perhaps from a feeling of relief, my lower abdomen suddenly started to ache. There was an outhouse in the field that
farmers seemed to use as they worked, for it was screened with straw
mats. As I crouched, the straw mats sheltered me below the waist, and I
looked up at the sky. Heedless of the disaster in Urakami, it was quietly

turning light purple. As I twisted my head around, I saw some pale stars.

The town was growing dark faster than the sky. Of course, no electric lights could be seen, and here and there smoke rose from fires as suppers cooked. Children who were in the schoolyard just a while before were gone. It was still lighter around the school than the flat houses, and the window glass shone, reflecting the red glow of the clouds which tarried in the western sky. Some of the glass seemed to have been damaged by the wind, for next to the shining panes were dark squares—like missing teeth.

The town was indeed peaceful. Moreover, I was crouching over a toilet pit dug in the middle of the farm. It was so big that one could almost swim in it. The farm wind felt pleasant on my bare bottom. "I want a peace that lets me relieve myself in the field," said a soldier once to my mother, a man home briefly before being transferred to another front. I agreed. The peace of defenselessness was good.

I had diarrhea. The watery stools were the color of squeezed grass. I thought it was because I had eaten uncooked pumpkin, but I learned later that it was a disturbance caused by radiation. According to the Nagasaki Medical School's atomic bomb first-aid report, this was a proleptic disturbance of the digestive organs. It stated:

> On the following day or so stomatitis began, the temperature rose, and the intake of food or drink became difficult. And yet on the whole no alarming symptoms existed at this point. We were relaxed about the patients' condition, therefore, but then such disturbances as loss of appetite and stomachache appeared, finally followed by diarrhea. The diarrhea was watery stools, sometimes containing mucus, and rarely, blood. Within a week to ten days after the attack of the disease, the patient died in 100 percent of the cases, despite all treatment.

After I returned to my lodgings, the diarrhea got worse. My room was on the second floor. The second floor toilet was linked to a receptacle downstairs. The watery stools that gushed downwards were so endless that it was almost scary. My condition was moving right toward death, with certain steps.

When I discovered that Junin-machi was safe, I returned the ten-yen note to the woman. She carefully spread the folded bill and put it in her purse, saying, "I will keep it then, because now this purse is my entire property." We parted on the hill. They went down the hill to search for an acquaintance in Nakagawa.

The mountain trail changed to stone steps, with houses on both sides. At the bottom of the stone steps was my high school. I wanted to see my teachers as quickly as possible. I wanted to tell them I was alive. I ran down the steps. Two students of Nagasaki Higher Commercial School were ahead of me, one of them supporting the other on his shoulder. The injured one had a wound in the leg. The bleeding had stopped, but white flesh was exposed.

Nakagawa and Narutaki-machi near N Girls' High School were high class residential areas. A genteel-looking woman in silk gauze slacks and a girl of about twenty were giving rice balls to passers-by. Seeing the two students, the girl offered them some food. "You've been through so much." They each took a rice ball, but did not eat them. Looking at the well in the garden, they asked for water. The girl put down her tray and ran to the well. The balls of white rice, then such a rare luxury, looked like shining jewels on the garden stone.

The older woman went up to the students, and started to dress the wounded leg with a towel. Nobody noticed me coming down behind them barefoot, so I passed them by. The woman probably thought I was not among the bombed; they didn't say *gokurosama* or any word of sympathy. I remember feeling somewhat disturbed. As I recall it, I laugh at my own meanness. I did not want to eat a white riceball—as the commercial school students did not eat them, I also had no appetite. What I wondered was how this family had enough rice to share with others at a time when people lived on scanty rations. More clearly, I envied them thinking, 'How nice that they can eat like this every day.' Even so, I had no appetite. I also remember thinking that women were kind only to men. I must be mean by nature. An intuitive response like that could only mean that I am of mean character.

Nagasaki Higher Commercial School and N Girls' School were separated by a street five meters wide. It was a concrete paved street covered with pebbles. It used to be so narrow that on a rainy day only one person with an umbrella could pass. That meant that two had to share one umbrella, and so the narrow alley became a matchmaker between the commercial school students and the high school girls. In one case love developed into a double suicide. Finally, the schools separated the boys and girls: the boys had to use the upper path above the stone steps of the Suwa Shrine, while the girls were to use the lower path. By our time, however, the street had become wider. After the war, encouraged by the tide of freedom and liberation and "The Green Mountains," a movie about youth which was wildly popular, we even teased commercial school students by calling their names as they passed in the street below our school, a four-storey reinforced concrete building standing close to the street. The wind of the bomb extended its lethal hand even to the Nishiyama area. The windows were all shattered, in the bathroom, too. Depending on the direction the rooms faced, the ceilings and walls were also torn off. Walls between classrooms had collapsed. It amused me to think how much more convenient the big room would be for whiling away a boring lecture.

The window glass lay shattered on the street in a thousand pieces. I had felt no qualms walking barefoot over the thorny trail of Mt. Konpira, but it required courage to tread on the glass-covered street. The school building was directly before me now. I looked up at the windows. The

iron frames, bent like bows, were open, some inward and others outward.
The way the windows on the same wall opened in different directions
was vivid testimony to the complex power of the wind. The classrooms
were dark and quiet.

Survivors of the bombed areas had the duty to report their survival so
they were first to return to their schools. If some of the students here
had returned, there should have been the noise of girls. Also if survivors
had reported back, the school would have formed first-aid teams led by
teachers, since the students had been stationed in factories in the center
of the bombed area. Teachers and remaining students should have been
directed to stand at the gate to meet wounded students returning to
school. None of these things happened. Strangely, when I was still in the
heart of the bombed area, I had not felt such a deep sense of disaster,
even when I stumbled over some of the countless dead bodies and seriously wounded lying on the ground. After leaving the bombed area and step-
ping into a peaceful byway of daily life, I gradually began to sense the
gravity of the event. The very tranquility of the school buildings and of
the houses now seemed to highlight the misery of Matsuyama-machi,
Urakami, and all of Nagasaki.

The regular students of N Girls' High School had been stationed at
the Ohashi Munitions Plant, except for fourth-year girls, who, with special course students, had gone to the Hamaguchi Factory of the Mitsubishi Steel Foundry, the factory nearest the target of the bombing. Some
had been sent to the factory in a tunnel at Michi-no-O; they were unhurt.

The death rate of students sent to the Hamaguchi Factory was high.
In the alumni directory, I find a page where nineteen out of thirty-six are
listed as dead. A dark line is drawn beside the name of each deceased student on the quiet page which fears to breathe. Under the name it says:
Date of death, August 9, 1945, atomic bomb. This is the case with seventy percent of the dead. The rest died by August 24th. When I turn the
pages to find an address, I always come to this page. I just close my eyes
and pray. When I see the names of those whose date of death is September, my heart aches, knowing how dreadful it must have been to live the
long days afterward.

The second term started a month late in October. There was a redis-
tribution of classes, and one class less in each grade. Each class had fifty-
two or fifty-three students, making four grades in the regular section,
and three in the special section. In other words, nearly four hundred
were dead.

I walked over the glass-covered street to school. Perhaps my tension
protected my feet, for I was not cut. Books and papers were scattered
over the teachers' room, but there was no teacher. The evening wind
blew in through torn doors, and whirled the students' papers about. The
tranquility after the destruction was unbearable. I called out from the
corridor, but no teacher came out of the room. The door to the school
master's room was open. Looking in, I saw him standing near the window

watching a special course student burn old newspapers in the corner of
the school yard.

He turned back when he noticed me, and patted my shoulder, saying,
"Thank goodness, you're all right." And looking me up and down,
"You're not wounded?" He asked if I had seen any other students. I
shook my head. Sighing deeply, he said, "It's impossible to find out who
is alive. All the teachers have gone to Urakami to help with relief. But so
many students return as corpses. It is just terrible." There were tears in
his eyes.

Those few who came back to school alive were badly wounded and
were tended by relatively strong students. The auditorium housed wounded students and outsiders as well, to its full capacity. There wasn't even
space to walk. "Do you really have no wounds? If you have any, get
some treatment, then go home to your mother quickly. Stay home until
you hear from us." So saying, he took down my address.

Mercurochrome was the only medicine they had. They poured it in
big bowls, dipped a towel in it, and applied it all over the body. The
school infirmary supply soon ran out. They then burnt newspapers in
the schoolyard, mixed the ashes with cooking oil, and pasted it over the
burns. I wonder what happened to those who received that treatment.

The Nagasaki Medical School report says, under the heading of "Fatal
Dose of Radiation," that diarrhea and other disturbances in the digestive
system were first thought to have come from eating pumpkins and other
things in the bombed area, but that they now believe the cause to be a
fatal amount of radiation received over the entire body. According to
this interpretation, the patient received more than the fatal amount of
secondary radiation in the bombed area, and became ill after a brief incubation period. Even if the patient had received the fatal amount, he
did not die immediately because atomic bomb radiation always had an
incubation period. However, since the radiation stayed in the body, no
treatment was effective. There was no difference noted between cases
with and without external wounds. The report adds that this sort of disease occurred most commonly among people who were in the area where
houses were destroyed by the explosion. The husband of the woman in
kasuri trousers frequently spat saliva while talking. As the blood oozed
from his gums he spat repeatedly, saying, "It feels so sticky." If the fatal
amount of radiation had entered his body, he should have died.

I left school and went to my lodging house in Junin-machi, going
along the main street with its many shops and houses. From afar the
town seemed to have escaped the attack, but it had been damaged after
all. Walls leaned into the street, as if bowing to each other. Nobody could
get their rain doors closed. They had to nail them, leaving space for entrance and exit. The rumor ran about that the remaining towns were going to be fired with incendiary bombs, and people were scattering to the
mountains and trenches to spend the night, while civilian defense corps

members stayed to watch the town. They had mounted a cordon at every corner and stopped all passers-by to ask their identity. The town appeared defiant, and people were questioned until they convinced the guards that they were innocent fugitives.

It was after eight o'clock when I arrived at my boarding house. When I washed my ash-covered hair the following day, sand filled the bottom of the basin. Together with the mud and sand, there were glass slivers... six of them. They had stuck in my braids. What shielded me almost completely from the devastating wind and flash of the explosion, I wonder? I should like to know exactly what went into creating such good fortune.

On the following day, August 10th, I met Inatomi who had come from Shimabara to join the relief teams. He came to find me in Gassenjo, where I had taken refuge. In the gentle sloping hills, famous for the flag festival, the residents of Junin-machi had taken refuge on the night of the 10th, convinced that their town was in danger of further attack. Inatomi had stopped at my lodging and found out that I had already gone there.

He and others had gone to Urakami on the morning of the 10th to attend the corpses. They left bleached bones untouched on the burnt field, but collected bodies burned black and naked white. They were placed in circles with the heads in the center, a practical way of laying out bodies that facilitated identification by relatives who came to look for their dead. It saved them from having to walk from one to another.

After working hard at this task, Inatomi had rested on the edge of the terraced field on a hill, and felt a cold shiver creep down his spine. The circles of dead bodies he had laid out with prayers looked to him like mildew that rots the earth.

Now lying on the slope beside me, Inatomi told me what it had been like in Urakami during the day. The night mist settled and my head felt cool. "Are you cold?" he asked. I shook my head to let him know I wasn't. He stretched out his arm and put my head on it.

One of the bodies Inatomi recovered was an N Girls' High School student. She had run from the munitions plant to Urakami, where she had fallen. She was lying supine on the scorching road. One of the two strands of her braided hair had come undone and her clothes had burnt away. The flesh of her limbs had partially come off, and occasionally her fingers twitched. She was still breathing, and had no wound on her face. Her skin had looked translucent like that of a wax doll. Her eyes had been half open.

Inatomi had taken off his jacket and put it on the girl's body. She had had a sneaker on one foot. Inside the sneaker her school and family name were written. Inatomi had torn off a piece of his towel, and written on it the girl's family name with a stick of charcoal picked up from the burnt field and dipped in water. He had wrapped it around the girl's wrist. Death was a matter of minutes. When he returned with water from the truck, she was already dead.

Her name was Araki. There were several Arakis in my grade. One of them was among the most lovely-looking girls in our grade, with wavy hair and translucent, porcelain-like skin. But this does not help identify the girl that Inatomi found. For after the bombing, all our skins grew translucent, like wax. The Araki I knew, I heard, was the only daughter of a local physician. I wonder if this girl was her.

The sky over Gassenjo was full of stars. Little stars flickered. Meeting Inatomi, I felt emotionally weak. The fragile light of the little stars reminded me of Araki and many of my friends. I thought of the helpless girls who had died without their fathers and mothers. For the first time I was tearful—amidst the countless deaths of Urakami, I had been an emotionless robot.

The sky over Urakami was still as red as the day before. "Are you cold?" Inatomi asked again. He was shivering. Suddenly he said, "Let's go to Brazil when the war is over." He had had enough of bombing and corpses. "I might not be able to walk," I answered, but he said, "I'll carry you on my back." I had barely made it walking to Gassenjo. I still had diarrhea. I slept curled up in his arms. I heard airplanes in the night sky. A member of the National Defense Corps walked around repeating in a low voice, "Enemy planes on the way."

When the sun began to rise in the morning, Inatomi brought me some water. "It's nice and cold because it's well water," he said, and put the rim of his iron hat to my lips. The leather sweat band inside the hat smelled like Inatomi. It was a sunny smell of the sweat of a healthy youth. Together with the water I drank Inatomi's smell. For the first time after the bombing, I felt I was alive.

I went down the hill of Gassenjo on Inatomi's back. Japanese silver leaf blossoms were in bloom in the shade earlier than their season. Inatomi's neck perspired in the strong sun. His sweat had no saltiness as I touched the tip of my tongue to his neck.

"Your sweat is sweet."

"Did you lick me?" he asked, and shaking me a little, added, "I'm dirty. I haven't had a bath."

"I am scared to go near the medical school," he said. "I feel guilty that I am alive. I wish some of the others were." And he went on down Gassenjo hill.

For a full week after that Inatomi had camped out in Gassenjo and recovered dead bodies.

My uncle, when he heard about the disaster in Nagasaki, left Isahaya early in the morning on the 10th to seek his son. "I'll try the medical school, though I don't know what to expect. When I let you know what I find, then you can decide what to do next," he said to my mother and aunt. Then he oiled his rusty bike and left.

In the afternoon, Isahaya filled up with wounded carried there in freight cars. The train was running as far as Ohashi, which was midway between Urakami and Michi-no-O. There was no station at Ohashi, but the train went right up to where the rails had been destroyed. Isahaya Station looked like a wholesale fish market. The badly wounded were laid out on the platform like skinned tuna. There were nowhere near enough people to tend them, so they just lay and waited on the sunny platform. Among them was Tayama from our school. She had a burn on her back, with glass slivers imbedded in it. She waited her turn for treatment, lying on her stomach on the burning concrete platform. "What really hurt was the sun," she told me later. "We were in direct sunlight and it was torture." Sunlight scorches the burns and the blood dries, pulling the flesh taut. The victim can feel the action of the sun piercing the wounds. 'Won't somebody come and pour some cold water on my back,' she kept wishing. Araki must have suffered the same pain.

My mother and aunt were among the many who put private concerns behind public ones and joined in as the entire women's association plunged into twenty-four hour first aid activities. When my mother went to the navy hospital to tend the wounded there, she saw Tayama and asked if I was safe. "I'm not sure," Tayama said hesitantly. She really didn't know, because she and I had worked in different sections. But my mother read into her evasiveness an indication that I was dead, and she collapsed on the floor.

My uncle returned late on the night of the 12th, dragging the bike. He sat down on the threshold. "It's all over, everything," he said. He opened a cloth in which small pieces of bone and ash were wrapped. He had inquired about his son of another medical student giving first-aid near the school. The boy said he wasn't sure, but added that my cousin had probably been at a lecture at the time of the bombing, and told him the room number. When his son had entered the college, my uncle used to make up various excuses to go there. Since he had attended school only up to the fourth grade, college was something new to him. He had learned his way around the campus and could guess which classroom to search in the destroyed building.

On the floor of the room were bones and ashes, nineteen separate heaps of them in a circle. It was as though each student had sat on the floor cross-legged. In the center were two bodies, now only bone and ash. They must be the professors, my uncle thought. Then he checked each pile of the outer circle. Carefully so that he wouldn't spread the ashes, he felt for teeth. His son had had bad teeth beginning in middle school, and had several gold caps.

"Your cavities devoured my money. Come on, open your mouth," he once showed the caps to my mother and others, recalling how much they had cost.

If he found those caps in the ashes, his son must certainly be dead. In one of the heaps of ash and bone, a grain of gold shone. My uncle picked up the molten and hardened grain, but that still did not convince him of his son's death. He sat down inside the circle, thinking that maybe his

son was not dead after all. When he checked the last heap, hope still lingering, he came upon his son's fountain pen. He recognized the strong
gold point of the German pen my father had given him when he entered
college. My uncle stroked the ashes with both hands. "So you died, so
you died," he cried, no longer withholding his tears.

My uncle picked up one of the bones of the person who looked like a
professor and put it in his kerchief. He also took a piece from the heap
next to the professor. He took one from each heap in the circle and put
them all in his kerchief. As he gathered the fragments of bone, he spoke
to his son, "I'll take you home with everybody."

Although he had found the gold pen point, my uncle still could not
give up. He walked among the debris, checking the bodies and the wounded. He asked students about his son. A few of them knew him, and their
answers coincided. His son's death then seemed certain. Later my uncle
found Inatomi in the burnt field, and Inatomi told him that I was safe.

From that day until the end of the war, he would not leave his room.
On August 15th we turned on the radio to hear the emperor's announcement of Japan's defeat. My uncle listened, biting his lips "Why didn't
you tell us all this sooner?" He said bitterly.

After the end of the war the emperor came to Isahaya. We lived with
my uncle then. "I want to see him," my sister said, starting to go, when
he grabbed her.

"Go if you want. But I'll never let you set foot in this house again.
Let's have that understood, everybody."

He made us close all the rain doors at midday, in the only way he
could express his anger and resistance.

The Nagasaki Medical School was completely destroyed: more than
850 people were killed, including the president, teachers and students.

When my uncle returned, my aunt and my mother then left home.
Leaflets were scattered around town declaring, "On the 13th we will
thoroughly destroy all the remaining towns. Citizens of Nagasaki must
quickly evacuate." When people whispered about this, it sounded plaus-
ible. So my mother walked twenty-five kilometers with my aunt, who
wanted to see where her son had died, while mother was trying to locate
me. She arrived at my boarding house at two in the morning of the 13th.
She lay down for an hour, and then put straw sandals on my feet though
I could hardly walk because of diarrhea. She tied them on my feet so
they would not slip off and said, "You look like Miyo." Cheerfully, she
sang a passage from a children's song, "Come spring, come quick; little
Miyo's starting to walk and wants to play outside."

An interesting rumor had it that this bomb worked only in dazzling
midday sun. The sun's heat made the heat of the bomb that much more
terrible, people said. We believed the rumor, too, for the flash from the
explosion was so hot.

We had to escape from Nagasaki before sunrise, so exactly at three
o'clock, my mother and I left Junin-machi. We reached Isahaya at two-

thirty in the afternoon. Though we walked without rest, it took us twelve hours. On the way, by sheer chance, we ran into Miss M on the beach at Kigitsu. She had been in Omura to attend a meeting on August 9th, and thus escaped the bombing. Miss T and Miss K were both killed.

"I feel very badly that I alone lived...I wish I could take their work too, and go on for all of us," she said to my mother. That day, she too had gone to Isahaya to search for students, and was on her way home. From the next day she planned to concentrate her search on the munitions plant.

Miss T died, her head split by a falling crane. Miss K, our Japanese classics teacher, seems to have lived an hour or two. She was found dead under a steel frame, holding the hand of a student who was also unable to move. One of my classmates died in the fire with one arm caught under the building. Someone heard her screaming, "Cut off my arm. Please!" The terror of the approaching fire must have been hell. Miss K's workplace did not catch fire. A small reprieve.

Their bodies were burnt by their colleagues. Miss M also died one month after we saw her at Kigitsu from secondary radiation. All her hair fell out and she became deranged a few days before her death, swinging her bamboo spear around in the air. Other teachers burnt her body in the vacant lot in front of the school gate. Pointing at the black soot that remained there, a friend said to me, "They burnt her there."

"Let's stay in good health until the war ends. Run when a B-29 comes."

These were the last words that I heard from Miss M. All three teachers were single, twenty-five or twenty-six. I wonder if they had ever been in love.

Miss T who was hit by the crane on the forehead was a beauty with brown eyes. She was tall and the only daughter of the family in a Buddhist temple. The day we left school to work in the factory, we had a physical examination. I was sent this way and that in the medical office, now for a red blood segmentation test, then for taking the temperature, and in the end I had a long wait in the X-ray room. As I stood nearly in tears in the corner of the room, Miss T smiled at me, saying that I did not have to worry. She held up the chain I wore around my neck and asked, "A charm?" It was a silver locket that my father had sent me and had little rubies on it.

"There is no picture in it." My flustered answer prompted my teacher to say, "You must have your boyfriend's picture inside. If you don't take it off, his face will show in your X-ray," she teased me. She had dimly brown eyelashes.

The war ended on August 15th, the 20th year of Showa. It was only one week after the atomic bomb. "Why didn't you tell us all this sooner?" My feeling about the surrender, too, is simply that.

One day after the end of the war, a young girl who worked at the town hall came in through our back gate. She asked my mother who was hanging out laundry for any old newspapers we might have. The town office was collecting old newspapers to use for medicine.

"They make medicine for burns out of newspapers. It works, you know." Then she noticed me.

"Is she the one who was exposed?" She looked at me and my mother thoughtfully, and then said, "The bomb this time, you know ... even those who get home safe all die, sooner or later. The bomb is made that way. I am so sorry."

The girl looked about two years younger than myself. She had not bothered to lower her voice, and was honestly sad. "Away with your nonsense! Get back to your office, quick," my mother yelled at her.

People were saying the same thing all over town, and it seemed to be true. Coffins kept passing our door. Many of the people who had commuted from Isahaya to factories in Nagasaki were now encased in unfinished wood coffins and carried by their families along the Honmyo River to the cremation ground.

The young man in the house at the back of us died, too. We heard the voice of a monk reciting a Buddhist scripture for him from early in the morning. He used to work at the iron foundry in Nagasaki. When he came home after the bombing unwounded, and talked to my mother over the fence, he looked happy: "I was lucky." Two or three days later, he developed a fever, lost his hair, had diarrhea of green stools, and died. People being housed in the Navy Hospital and schools died, too, one after another, and they all got diarrhea of green stools. Many died insane like Miss M. Perhaps it was because of the horror of the 9th.

It was weird when your hair began to fall, in great bunches, even at the slight turn of the neck. When it started to come out, I felt that death was near. I combed my hair every morning and checked the amount of fallen hair—surely it was increasing daily. Every day, I rounded it into a bun and showed it to my mother.

"It's autumn. That's why," she said pretending unconcern. One morning the comb disappeared from the mirror stand. No comb was left on my sisters' small mirror stand, either, for they had hidden all the combs. I was unkempt for a month from that day. I tied up the bottom of my braids very tightly and left them like that for a month. I was weak and had no appetite. Daily I lost more and more strength, until my head started to feel heavy. When I sat straight, my head weighed so heavily on my shoulders that they could hardly bear it. My arms and legs felt equally heavy and I was comfortable only when I was lying down. All day I lay there lazily. It seemed that my little sister had been told not to bother me, for she only watched me from a distance. My big sister also was gentle. Normally they were self-centered, but now they served me at my will.

One day as I happened to look at my arm, I saw a red spot about two millimeters in diameter, then I noticed a considerable number of them on the outside of my arm from the wrist up. The red spot was around the root of a hair, and the flesh there was coming off. It was deep red close to the root. Since it itched, I scratched the area with my nails, and the hair came off with softened fat. It was infected.

Similar spots formed on my legs, too, but none on my body. They were confined only to the part of my arms which had been exposed on the day of the bombing, and the area under the black slacks. In my case at least it was perfectly clear. Not a single spot appeared on the upper part of my arms that had been covered by my short sleeves. On my legs, the infection spread from the centers of the red spots up to the elastic band of the white calico underwear. In the human system, the digestive organs proved the most sensitive to radiation in the case of Nagasaki, but the roots of hair also reacted strongly. Infection is explained as a result of loss of physical strength and decrease of white blood cells, but how curious that my infection appeared only in areas not protected by white cotton, if indeed the cause is internal.

If I had had a blood test then, the white blood cell count might have been as low as two or three thousand. A few years ago it was down to 3,600 when I was checked at the regular examination of bomb victims. I received a letter at that time indicating that I needed a closer examination. I feared death then more intensely than when I faced it so directly at age fourteen. By then I had a little son and prayed fervently, 'I don't want to die now.'

The infection was bad. When I changed position, the pain concentrated around the lymph glands. It was hot in September. My sister stayed away from me saying that I smelled. It was not only the infected spots that smelled, but my hair also had an odor, for I had not washed it for a month. It had itched the first ten days, but after that I had grown used to it. I had lice nesting in my hair. I could feel them run through it, like silk threads being gently yanked. They increased so much that some of them started to crawl down my neck. My older sister could stand it no longer so she came in and cut the elastic off my braids. My hair's going to come out ... I turned to my mother wailing.

"When it falls, it falls; when one dies, one dies," said my sister, giving me no quarter. She had pampered me for a month and had had enough.

"Don't. This child may really die," said my mother, unwittingly revealing her fear. My sister immediately responded: "That's right. She may really die. But when? Someday? Someday I will die, too. I've had enough of her selfishness." My little sister was peeping in from behind the screen door. She was the greatest victim of my disease, for I had used her like one of my own limbs.

"Yes, I think so, too," she agreed briefly with my big sister. The glory of my narrow escape from death, which I thought would last the rest of my life, was finally denied by both my sisters.

When a patient expected to die in a few days lives on, the people

around her become tired of waiting. If you are going to die, die quickly,
they begin to wish. When I discovered this impatience in my sisters, I felt
like dying just to satisfy them. That's just my nature. But my hair did
not fall out after all—a cupful of lice and a heap of hair in my hands
were the month's total.

About that time a letter arrived, stuck in a cheap brown envelope.
The tip of the pen had split and scratched the paper, spotting the envelope with drops of ink. It was addressed to me and on the back was the
imprint of the rubber seal of the factory where I had worked. Inside I
found a printed greeting of a few lines and a postal money order. It was
my pay for the three months I had worked there. The total was 18 yen.

"I wonder if the girls who died were only paid 18 yen, too," my
mother said sympathetically from the kitchen, the western sun beginning to stream in the window.

The tuition at my high school was 7 or 8 yen a month at that time.
We had to pay it even when we were sent off to work in the factories.
This was our way of "serving the country"—paying tuition that was
more than what we earned. I wonder how the loss and gain should be cal-
culated. In any case, the 18 yen can pay for flowers if I die. It is not
enough to buy expensive Western flowers, but it will fill the coffin with
nameless flowers of the field. I would at least like a funeral with lots of
flowers as becoming to a girl. When I die, buy flowers for me with that
18 yen, I said half jokingly. My mother, who was steaming sweet potatoes, became really angry and said, "I won't spend good money on a
child who dies!"

I heard later that 52 yen was given for each student who died in the
bombing, from where, I don't know. Maybe the factories, maybe the
country paid for those lives. Either way, how very handy to be able to
measure life by money. It makes it a lot easier to know and behave ac-
cordingly. If I die now, the country will pay 16,000 yen for my funeral.
These death payments are earned for "special atomic bomb victims."
But you have to do more than just die. To get paid you have to get auth-
orized first as a bona fide atomic bomb victim.

A "special atomic bomb victim" means someone who has obtained a
"special atomic bomb victim health certificate," which is granted to
those who come under Article 6, numbers 1 to 5 of the Atomic Bomb
Medical Care Enforcement Regulations. I am a "special number 1 atomic bomb victim." This category covers those persons and fetuses who
were within three kilometers of the epicenter when the bombing occured.
It also includes some "special areas," which are places where the black
rain fell, but Isahaya did not qualify.

To get the 16,000 yen after your death, someone has to fill out an application for the payment of funeral expenses, and take that, along with
a medical certificate of death, a void resident card, a special atomic bomb
victim health certificate and a seal to the proper authorities. I intend to
leave a will saying, please buy flowers with the 16,000 yen. That's

enough for eighty tulips, even in winter when they are 200 yen each. What a beautiful funeral that will be. If that is more than I deserve, radishes will do. Just awhile ago it would have been enough for eighty large ones, but while writing this, the price has gone up. Now it will buy only fifty-three radishes.

People used to say that persimmon leaves are effective in curing atomic bomb disease, that they purify the poison and heal the infection. Using a bamboo pole, my mother beat down the leaves of a sweet persimmon tree in the yard. It was September, and too early for the leaves to fall so they were still dark green. The big ones held onto their desire to grow young shoots. As my mother whacked away at the tree, the branches bent and leaves scattered in all directions. She gathered them up carefully and washed them. In just enough water to cover them she boiled them patiently for a long time over firewood, until the green juice turned brown and then black. My mother filled a teacup with the juice and brought it over for me to drink. The smell of bitter persimmon leaves was special and the taste was so bitter that my chin twitched.

"I can't," I said, and handed the cup back to her. She looked at me sadly, "You won't get better." My mother's face was harder for me to bear than anything else. When I finally forced myself to drink it, she gave me a spoonful of white sugar, looking happy. Sugar then was a luxury kept for special occasions, and there was some rust from the can in it. The rusty taste was good. My mother could have mixed it into the persimmon juice, but she didn't, insisting that the more bitter it tasted, the more effective it would be.

The branches of our persimmon tree were bare in less than a week. My mother even went out to get sick leaves blown down the street by the wind. It put her in good spirits to be able to come back with a lot of them.

"You have to get better quick," she said, and washed the dirt away from the leaves at the well. The leaves turned deep green, and even the brown sick leaves shone in the bamboo sieve when they were washed. They looked so full of life; how could I possibly fail to recover if I drank juice from those dark, shiny leaves.

It had no effect. Another rumor had it that *dokudami* weed was good. My mother went to the bank of the Honmyo River, or searched the furrows in the field for this plant. She did not bother to dry it in the shade but boiled it as it was. The juice turned the same color as the persimmon juice, but it tasted flat, and felt heavy and unpleasant in the stomach. When it proved useless taken orally, my mother made me wash my body with it.

I would pat the infected areas with the *dokudami* extract. It stung the broken skin, perhaps because it is an herb, and pus fell into the washbasin. If I pressed the towel too hard over my exposed red flesh to wipe off the water, the towel stuck to the wound and it bled. When scabs formed over the raw places, there was no medicine to protect them. We didn't even have any bandages. When I sat down, the sores touched the tatami, and if I stood up quickly, the scabs came off, sticking to the mat. Then that area would get infected again. The same cycle repeated itself.

It was Takano who took pity on me and procured some medicine from an American doctor stationed in Obama. Carefully taking something wrapped in a sheet of ruled paper from his chest pocket, he produced three white pills. I was to take one every six hours, so my mother set the alarm clock and gave me the pills exactly on schedule. In ten days, the infection stopped, and yellow scabs covered the wounds.

I will never understand how the antibiotic could cure my infection if it was caused by the loss of white blood cells and physical strength. No matter how many times I hear it explained, I find it as odd as seeing green leaves growing on a tree which has rotted away at the roots.

On September 23rd, Inatomi died. It was a cool day, washed by a cold wind from the Ariake Sea. A typhoon was approaching, and the sea spreading out at the mouth of the Honmyo River glittered like lead. On days when cool breezes blew, the heat of the infection subsided and I felt good. Also, no new infection had occurred since I took Takano's medicine. I was watching the flow of the clouds, leaning against a post in the corridor facing the yard. My mother, returning from digging sweet potatoes, said, "I hear Inatomi-san is in the hospital." Because of a con- tinued high fever, he had gone to the hospital just that morning.

In the early afternoon I went to see him, carried in a cart. Although my infection was healing, it started to hurt whenever I walked, so I rode in the cart when I had to go out. Inatomi looked better than I had ex- pected, and waved, "Hi!" when mother and I came in. We were given only ten minutes visiting time by the nurse. His eyes were bloodshot from fever, and he was breathing hard. His condition was not as good as it first appeared, and as I watched him, I realized that his jaw was weak. He could not chew his food well, nor could he clearly pronounce vowels. He spoke with his lips half open. The cause of his fever was not known.

"It's lack of salt. If I eat hot rice gruel with a lot of sesame seeds and salt, I will get better quickly," he said lightly.

"We are really going to Brazil, okay?" he said looking at both me and my mother.

"I may not be able to walk," I said, repeating what I had said at Gas- senjo. Inatomi laughed.

"I will carry you on my back. May we, please, M'am?" My mother smiled, neither yes or no. I left after promising to heat fresh seaweed on rice paper, crush it with my palms, and mix it with sesame seeds and salt to make an extra good mix for him. I developed a fever on returning home, for it had been a long time since I had been out. Inatomi died that night.

At eleven o'clock at night, September 23rd, the rain that announces a typhoon had started to fall. The cause of his death was atomic bomb disease from secondary radiation.

In October 1945, the second term started, one month late. The opening assembly began with a memorial ceremony for the dead. The physician had told me to stay in bed, but I insisted on going no matter what. So I went, accompanied by my mother, and we attended the ceremony in the auditorium, with a huge hole in the ceiling above us. A chandelier hanging from the broken ceiling clinked as the wind touched its milky ornaments. On the wall behind the stage were all the names of teachers and students who had died in the bombing. They were closely written on five rolls of paper which stretched from one side of the stage to the other. How many dozens of names were there on each roll?

A table covered with a white cloth became a humble altar, bearing offerings of home-grown persimmons, still-unripened figs, green oranges, sweet potatoes, and flowers from the field. The iron frames of the building were exposed, and we could see the blue autumn sky. A refreshing breeze blew in.

Those of us who had survived the bomb sat in the chairs. Half of the students were bald—bald and dressed in sailor's uniforms they sat. Girls' heads should be covered with rich black hair, but now they were like nuns' heads, or worse, for the head of a nun has life about it. Those girls' heads were lifeless and sick. On either side of the hall sat the teachers and parents of the deceased students.

The recitation of the Buddhist scripture began. The schoolmaster sat motionless with his eyes closed and his fists tightly clasped. A mother in *mompe* trousers bent over and broke into tears. Fathers were all staring at the ceiling. Surviving students felt guilty to be there. The suppressed sobbing of mothers pierced our bodies.

Each home room teacher read out the names of her lost students, saying every name with sad affection. Thin smoke rose from burning incense sticks and the autumn wind blew in a ruffled the smoke. Then the students gathered there, still living, sang a song of mourning for their friends killed by the bomb.

Several students who had attended the ceremony died later. One friend who had married and had children died suddenly one morning from a bomb disease. Sometimes I still sing the same dirge, to mourn for the youth of all of us.

> Spring flowers, fall leaves, will return each year.
> Where are the dead—we call, and we call
> But they do not return.
> Ah! Our teachers. Our friends. Hear our ritual today.

There is a beautiful line at the end of an American documentary film on the atomic bomb:

... Thus, the destruction ended ...

—translated by Kyoko Selden

David Ray
FOR HARRY S. TRUMAN IN HELL

Your rusty Chrysler was advertised in the *K. C. Star*.
I called but was put off by the five thousand price
though the man admitted chickens had roosted in it
three decades and he had only lately found out you owned it,
drove it to the store a few times and in a parade.
I'd always hated you because you said you'd lost no sleep
over those children of Hiroshima, then sent the bombers back
to wipe out Nagasaki and yet I admired your desk-top phrase
THE BUCK STOPS HERE, and your unflappable sweet smirk,
rivalled by those great ones, Jimmy Stewart, Glenn Ford,
    Henry Fonda.
Once I took my mother and her retired army cook husband
to your museum where were displayed all
those presents you got as President, including
golden tea service from the Shah and a Turkey carpet hung
across a wall and well-lit, and down the hall
endless movies were shown in a little theatre—
your campaign whistle stops back when we had trains
with black balconies on their rears. Buxom Bess
was with you and you were unpretentious, just an average
guy from Missouri, the Show Me State. In the White House
you played just one tune on the piano, Missouri Waltz.
Once Lauren Bacall sat above you with legs crossed
while you grinned. By then we boys in backyards
had mourned F.D.R., had heard over the radio his caisson roll.
TV was still a fantasy—that ancient crone
who kept ten parrots told us they'd show her pictures soon
on the radio, soon as the war was done. She pointed to
two loose wires where they'd hook it up but we were sure
she was the fool with two wires loose. But neither would
our high school brains have grasped
that men with good minds stood in the desert, placed their bets
on whether they would blow the planet up or just New Mexico.
Therefore once when no one looked I stood above your grave
and thought I should be Gulliver, who put out fires with pee
in Lilliput—for I thought I saw the fires of Hiroshima

58

rage still in grass near your giant stone, saw frozen shadows
of those thousands just as they were caught forever
in the concrete of five bridges spanning the River Kyobashi.
But the F.B.I. watched, no doubt: *this* was *their* sacred spot.
Strange world! A man can go to jail for pissing on a grave
and yet a *great* one murders thousands, no penalty at all,
not for you who sent a naked man screaming with his eyeball
in his hand, who blackened thousands, tore breasts off
a beauty so they bled like pomegranates. Children nursed
their mothers' corpses to drink the milk of death.
Hair of the streetcar dead stood straight from fear.
A hand uplifted burned with blue flames through its fingers.
A squad of soldiers marching became a little ash and trickling
        flakes.
Through whorls of fire the black rain fell. And you were proud
as if good deeds would never end and we who followed
would praise your name and hold it sacred in our hearts.

William Stafford
INCIDENT

They had this cloud they kept like a zeppelin
tethered to a smokestack, and you couldn't see it
but it sent out these strange little rays
and after awhile you felt funny. They had this
man with a box. He pointed it at
the zeppelin and it said, "Jesus!" The man
hurried farther away and called out,
"Hear ye, hear ye!" Then they coaxed
the zeppelin down into the smokestack
and they said, "We won't do that any more."
For a long time the box kept shaking its head,
but it finally said, "Ok, forget it." But, quietly,
to us, it whispered, "Let's get out of here."

Joseph Bruchac
WAHSAH ZEH (War Dance)
—AS LONG AS THE GRASS

Then Old Man spoke to the people.
"Go and hide in our Mother," he said.
"The wind which comes will blow away your breath.
The rain which comes will burn your flesh.
Go and hide in our Mother," he said.

A cool morning in April,
I drive to work thinking.
The tiny fists of buds begin
to swell on trees beside the road.
The sap in the maple buckets turns yellow.
The grass edges its way to green.
These are things which can be seen,
but other forces touch my life,
more invisible than air itself
or greed which masters human hearts.

Woman who fell from the sky
    Grandmother
Woman who fell from the sky
    Grandmother

Who held the seeds of plants in her hand
Who fell to new earth on Turtle's back
Who held the good seeds of plants in her hand
Who fell to this Earth on Turtle's back

You, who gave birth, your children need you
You, who gave life, your grandchildren need you
You, who brought birth, your grandchildren need you
You, who brought life, your children need you

Less than 500 miles from here,
men and women work calmly near the Nuclear Plant.
They tell themselves, as they tell reporters,

that nothing is wrong, that American know-how
which sends rockets streaking, scrawls of chalk
across black space to distant planets,
can always control the monsters it creates.

They do not know the stories
of this Earth they live on,
have never heard of the Evil Mind
Longhouse People tell of in winterlodge tales.

They have never seen the Kinzua Dam
cover good corn land of the Seneca Nation,
graves of leaders, George Washington's word.

They have never seen Smallpox
smile from gift blankets,
seen beaches of Maui, Kaui and Hawaii
covered with 400,000 bodies,
limbs burned by the fire of western disease . . .
as the Mandan, Arikara enter the Sweat Lodge
and the pustules swell, swell up like a bubble
of radioactive hydrogen trapped
within the dome of a safe reactor.

And perhaps this nation knows no myths
and even the story of Mary Shelley's haunted flesh
means nothing more than a way to hold children
for an hour before the pale eye of commerce
whose rainbow dreams hypnotize away
all humanity which does not exist for profit.

And somehow
no one knows how
Karen Silkwood's car
goes off the road.
A thousand papers flutter about her,
they are the white swans who flew up from the water
to catch the woman who fell from the sky.
They are too late.

62

And somehow
no one knows how
when police arrive
the papers are gone
and the men of Kerr-McGee sleep soundly
and the red earth of Oklahoma
is Karen Silkwood's burying ground.

And somehow
no one knows how
there was plutonium contamination
in her bathroom
plutonium contamination
in her bedroom
plutonium contamination
in her food and perhaps
say the men at the Nuclear Plant
whose safety practices she had condemned
she intended to contaminate herself
to gain publicity
this is what they say
the men at Kerr-McGee
and do they sleep soundly?

This is a song of quiet anger,
of anger which will be quiet no longer.

If only, perhaps, they could watch just one finger
of their left hand begin to decay half an inch,
a tenth of an inch each time they absorbed
enough to shorten a life,
start the crazy quilt proliferation of leucocytes.
If only *that*, instead of numbers,
of dosimeter readings which measure a "4"
which they say is only as much radiation
as one would get from 200 chest x-rays.
Then they set "5" as the number safe
to absorb in one month.

Madame Curie,
patron saint
of luminous watches,
we honor you.

Madame Curie,
held up to me,
heroine of my childhood,
we honor you.

Madame Curie,
limbs thin as sticks,
hair falling out,
we honor you.

Madame Curie,
face a pale candle,
blown out by leukemia,
we honor you.

Because the spirit cannot be seen,
is it not there?
Tell me it is not there
when you see the body
of a human
which no longer holds it.
Tell me that breath is less important
than the color of skin, the clothing you wear,
the whiteness of teeth in a "sex-appeal" smile.

Woman who comes walking
    Grandmother
Woman who comes walking
    Grandmother

You wear a dress of white Buffalo Skin
You walk to us with visible breath
You wear the dress of white Buffalo Skin
You walk to us from four directions

White Buffalo Woman
White Buffalo Woman
White Buffalo Woman
White Buffalo Woman

You bring the Pipe,
the heart of the people
You bring the stone
the blood of the people
You bring the stem
the plants of the earth
You bring the tobacco
breath of the Creator

And of those who saw you coming
one whose heart was good
brought back life to the people,
one whose heart was bad,
who saw your body and not the beauty
of the gift you carried
who looked at you as corporations
look at the Earth, at the coal of Black Mesa,
at the oil shale of the Crow Reservation
at the North Slope of Alaska,
that one, that other one
fell to the Earth
fell to the Earth
to the Earth as bones
and worms crawled among his bones.

This is a song of anger
for the dream they are killing
is not just my own.
They eat the earth from beneath the feet
of our grandchildren's grandchildren.

Satanta, the great Kiowa chief,
said it more than a hundred years ago.
"You cut down the trees, kill the Buffalo,

you make the streams filthy
so that even you have no water to drink.
Are you people crazy?"
And in answer the army officers spat at his feet.

Let them kill themselves?
Is that what you say?
But the grave they dig is American,
a giant economy size, a family model,
the only product manufactured for profit
which does not have built-in obsolescence.

The half-life of radioactive wastes
manufactured by our nuclear plants
can be measured in tens of thousands of years.
The glaciers returned to the poles
but these will remain, faithful through the ages.

It is as if the poison which killed a Roman emperor
stayed in the air until today, killing every person
who breathed it.

It is as if the spear which wounded the side
of Christ still hung, invisible, on the hill
of Golgotha, goring every living creature
which came close to that place.

It is as if the stone Cain hurled
against his brother were orbiting, a tiny evil moon,
striking down guilty and innocent from that time on.

And the Sun
watches

We do not see him.
We do not accept the gift offered freely.
There is no profit in solar power.
There is power in the reactor's poison.
There is profit in oil, in coal, in the rape

of our Mother to bring forth her black blood
and bones burning in factories, smoke choking sky
acid rain weeping into mountain lakes,
trout dying, trees dying, the water bitter.

And Grandmother Moon
fills up the night,
Grandmother Moon fills even our dreams
with the light of Sun
the light they have not seen

A man is about to leap from a ledge.
He is not trying to kill himself.
He swears he will be able to fly.
Some believe him, some know
he is a fool, but no one stops him.
They all stand by
as he leaps to the crowded street below,
even though, strapped to his back
as if it could lift him into flight,
is a case of dynamite.

This poem is a poem of anger.
This poem calls back those of the past.
It calls back Powhatan,
it calls back Madakwando
it calls back Pomtiac
it calls back Tecumseh
it calls back Dragging Canoe
it calls back Osceola
it calls back Captain Jack
it calls back Cochise
it calls back Chief Joseph
it calls back Dull Knife
it calls back Satank
it calls back Looking Glass
it calls back Crazy Horse
it calls back Sitting Bull

Tatanka Iyotake
Tatanka Iyotake
Tatanka Iyotake
Tatanka Iyotake

It calls all those whose spirits never left us
It calls all those whose spirits never left us
It calls all those whose spirits never left us
It calls all those whose spirits never left us

GER O NI MO
GER O NI MO
GER O NI MO
GER O NI MO

There are no mountains in which to hide
from the rain which will fall.
No one can dodge the bullets of this gun
which kills even the hand which fires it.

This poem calls back Ayontwatha.
This poem calls back the Peacemaker.
This poem will say the sacred names.
It calls all those who love the Earth,
calls both living and dead on Turtle's back.

It calls the Bear Mothers
It calls Gluskabe
It calls Grandmother Spider
It calls Manabozho
It calls Coyote
It calls Moon, our Grandmother
It calls the Manitous
It calls the Thunderbird
It calls the Kachinas
It calls the Thunderers

HE NO
HE NO

HE NO
HE NO

Grandfathers
wash the Earth
Grandmothers
wash the minds
of those who do not believe in circles

Grandfathers, take them,
make their minds straight
Grandmothers, take them,
make their hearts good.

Listen, all of us who love our children
Listen, all of us who love our land
Listen, all of us who love our parents
Listen, all of us who love our friends

All of us are "Indian" now
The treaty not made is the only one
which might never be broken.
It promises waste, it promises death
for as long as the rivers run
for as long as the grass shall grow

We must answer: No.
We must answer: No.
We must answer: No.
WE MUST ANSWER: NO!!!!

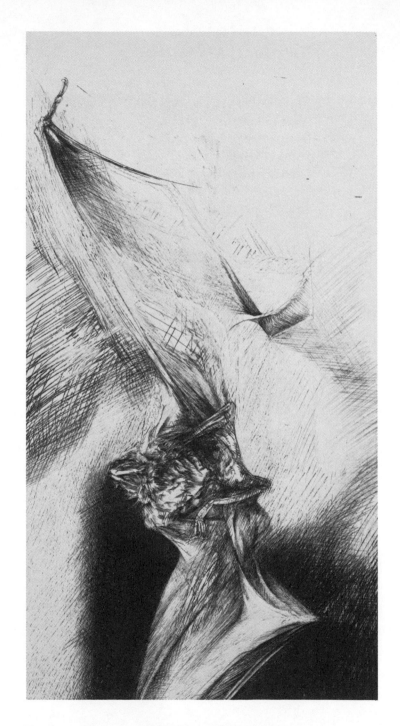

Gay Rogers / intaglio print

Robert M. Chute
NATURAL SELECTION

From tests over Pacific atolls
cruel light rouses birds
from palms silhouetted
sharp against an artificial dawn.
Dark birds, turning light to heat,
feathers burning, inscribe
smokey parabolas into the sea.
Only white birds fly on tonight.

There was a precise time
when it became important
to be a white bird.
At time zero we might know
what accident may have saved us.

Don Dolan / pen & ink

Margaret Randall
MARCH 6, 1982

All last week you preened before the mirror,
viewing emerging breasts, then covering them
with gauze-thin blouse
and grinning: getting bigger, huh?
The week before you wore army fatigues
leveling breasts and teenage freckles,
tawny fuzz along your legs.
A woman. Beginning.
Today you don fatigues again.
Today you pack knapsack and canteen,
lace boots over heavy socks
and answer the call Reagan and Haig have slung
at your 12 years.
Yours and so many others . . .
kids 14, 15, 18, so many others who will go
and some of them stay, their mothers shouting
before the Honduran Embassy: "Give us
our sons' bodies back, give us back their bodies!"
At least that.
All last week you preened before the mirror,
moving loose to new rhythms
long weekend nights, Junior High math. Sunday beach.
Today you went off to the staccato of continuous
        news dispatches
and I, in my trench, carry your young breasts
in my proud and lonely eyes.

Managua, Nicaragua

Lee Patton
CROSSING THE MISSILE ZONE

In cowgirl casinos
in towns where all the children have birth defects,
you poke at your queasy square of hash browns,
certain only toothpicks are free.
The crosseyed cashier here at the Last Chance Cafe
has a deaf and one-armed mutant they slapped to life
for this: to exist, drugged, mute, drooling, blind.
This momma's your age, born the year
her momma watched the Army Corps detonate at dawn.
"Hell, they spit South Nevada across the sky."

The billboard Indian
rusting on the ridge points east,
aiming you over two lanes of tar
rising to Nevada's only paradise:
God's dawn behind a pine summit
where Basques still tend sheep
on green gashes in eroded hills,
once islands in a prehistoric sea
where nothing swam but brine
and doomed, golden women.
All you can get on the radio's
a prayer for the Prince of Peace
brought to you by killers, Jesus,
killers.

Judith Waring
ON THE BRINK

ON THURSDAY, March 29, 1979, *The Morning News* of Wilmington, Delaware, where I live, ran the following headline: NUCLEAR PLANT SPEWS RADIATION. The nuclear plant is the Three Mile Island plant, just south of Harrisburg, Pennsylvania. I scan the article and read quotes that say, "... the company does not believe level constitutes danger to health and safety of public," and "There is absolutely no danger of a meltdown," and forget about the whole business.

On Friday evening, I am looking forward to watching the final episode of "Dallas," the nighttime soap, on television. My husband, Bob, has just removed the old, debilitated electric stove from its greasy niche in the wall of the kitchen. A new gas stove waits in the adjacent family room where the delivery men had put it that morning. The children, Adam, sixteen, and Ann, fourteen, turn on the tv set in the family room about 7:00 only to find their program is pre-empted by dire-sounding reports from Three Mile Island.

Wilmington is seventy miles southeast of Three Mile Island. The prevailing winds come from the northwest, putting it in direct line for fallout of airborne radioactivity.

The commentators are quoting Nuclear Regulatory Commission officials as saying a meltdown is now possible. One government spokesman says there were "uncontrolled bursts of radiation" early this morning. "A thirty millirem/hour reading was taken south of the plant. I did not expect the radiation levels to be that high," says a NRC spokesman. But a plant official says the release was intentional and that such releases would continue for up to five days.

The phone rings. It is a friend of Ann's. She and Ann had plans to spend the night together but the friend's aunt, cousins, grandmother and great-grandmother arrived without warning just before dinner. They have left their homes in York, Pennsylvania (ten miles due south of Three Mile Island), for the safety of Wilmington. They will spend the weekend. The girls' overnight is cancelled.

The commentators are explaining that if a meltdown occurs, thousands of square miles would be contaminated from radioactive material released into the atmosphere. No one says how far it would extend. I grow apprehensive. As I clean out the empty stove space, I feel my heartbeat throb in my throat.

Bob and Adam move the new stove into place. Before the stove was delivered, Bob went to the store and measured it so he could have the gas line all ready to hook up when the stove came. Now he discovers his calculations are three-quarters of an inch off and swears at the pipe. Usually I am elated at the prospect of a new appliance, hopeful that it will solve all the problems generated by the deterioration of the old one.

But tonight I am not. The idea of a new stove seems absurd in the face
of a possible nuclear disaster. I hover between the kitchen and the family room, hoping for definite news, news that will make clear what I
have to do. But none comes.

Instead, there is word of a bubble in the reactor vessel which is hind-
ering efforts to cool down the reactor. John Comey of the Pennsylvania
Emergency Management Agency is quoted as saying earlier, "Businesses
in Harrisburg appear to be releasing employees. People are leaving the
Harrisburg area."

Pennsylvania's governor, Dick Thornburgh, issued an advisory early
this afternoon that pregnant women and preschool children living within five miles of the plant should evacuate the area. "Schools will be
closed," he said. "There is no reason for panic." The evacuation is
based on "my belief that an excess of caution is best . . . ." Those living
within ten miles of the plant had been advised earlier in the day to stay
indoors.

I think about leaving. I did not fill the tank of my car today. The
morning paper warned of limited gasoline supplies: "Delaware drivers
looking for gasoline this weekend will find 'no gas' signs at some stations, and a growing number of Sunday closings, to conserve dwindling
supplies. The closings and reduced hours are expected to create lines at
stations still operating."

I ask Bob if his car has gasoline. He says he just filled it. But that is
slight comfort. His car is eleven years old and has been missing badly
for several weeks. Its driver has to double pedal, keeping one foot always on the accelerator, even when stopped, to prevent stalling. It chug-
a-lugs gasoline.

By now, Bob has the stove installed and we talk about what to do
with the old one. I will make some calls on Monday to various agencies
which might use it. As I say this, I wonder if I will be here on Monday.
I feel an impatience over these discussions of routine matters, unable to
concentrate. We have a cup of tea to celebrate the new stove.

By now, my anxiety is non-specific and generalized. I worry about
the gas line. This is the first time Bob has done any plumbing by himself. I ask him to shut off the gas to the new stove. In the morning he
will check all the new joints in the pipes for leaks, but tonight I cannot
trust them. It's as though I am trying to find some concrete steps to
take to make my family safe for the night, and this is the only one I can
think of.

"Dallas" is not going to be shown so we go to bed. I sleep fitfully,
waking often in an adrenalin-spiked state of watchfulness.

Saturday morning, Bob and I rise early. He turns on the gas to the
stove so I can cook pancakes and make coffee. He brings in the paper
and reads it while I make breakfast. The headline says: CONDITION IS
CALLED STABLE AT PLANT, and underneath: Concern Grows Over Meltdown. We eat the pancakes and linger over coffee. I remind Bob to

check for gas leaks in the cellar.

At about eight-thirty, as we are cleaning up, the phone rings. It must be a good friend, I think, one who knows we get up early on Saturdays. Bob answers. "Hi, Jan," he says. It is a friend from Friends (Quaker) Meeting where we are members. Jan is a patent attorney. He escaped from Hungary in 1956. He is calling Bob for advice. I hear Bob say he has decided to believe the officials in charge and has assumed there is no danger to us in Wilmington. He takes the phone into the hall and shuts the door. I can no longer hear.

Bob is a physicist. He is a solid state physicist, currently working with pigments. He doesn't feel like much of an expert in this present crisis. But to a patent attorney, any physicist is an expert.

When he hangs up in a few minutes, he tells me about the call. Jan's family is considering leaving town. Jan has work that he must do here so he will stay, but he is going to help his wife, Margaret, and their two girls leave. They do not trust the authorities. Margaret heard alarming news this morning about the bubble in the reactor vessel. Jan pointed out that if we wait until the authorities advise us to leave, we won't make it. There will be too big a crush. He said Margaret and the girls, if they went, would stay away until the danger was over. If we didn't see them at Meeting in the morning, it would mean they had left. Bob said he and Jan discussed which direction to go. Bob advised going west.

A wave of fear floods over me. I can feel my elbows go weak. We talk about it. Margaret sometimes overreacts to situations. This time she will be either right or foolish. I say I hope she's foolish.

We turn on the radio. The news is of the bubble. There is still talk of a possible meltdown. An NRC spokesman said, "The sealed reactor vessel, which should always be full of cooling water, apparently developed a pressurized bubble at the top. Unless attempts to reduce pressure are handled carefully, the bubble could expand, leaving the tops of the fuel rods exposed instead of under water. That would cause the rods to overheat and melting could occur."

I go find the morning paper again. I look for news of a strike by United Airlines machinists, threatened for Friday at midnight. There is a small notice on page three. It reads, "United Airlines, the nation's largest air carrier, suspended all flights through April 9 late yesterday." The web grows tighter, I think. No gasoline, an airline strike and a nuclear disaster. I am really frightened.

Adam and Ann show up for breakfast. Adam says he needs a car to go downtown for the day. He is helping a repertory group fix up an unused theater in a large center-city church. Ann grumbles about all the homework she has and about her piano recital on Sunday, for which she feels unprepared. "I don't even want to be in it," she says. I tell Adam he may have my car but warn him not to let the gas tank get much below half full. Tomorrow I will be driving Ann to her recital at the university, twenty miles away, and don't want to run out of gas with no stations open.

In truth, I don't want Adam to leave. I want all my chickens in the nest in case we have to make a hasty exit. But I don't tell him so.

I busy myself with the week's laundry. I don't know what to do with my fear and hope that keeping busy might help. But I find myself doing loads in order of priority, in case we need clean clothes in a hurry. The first load contains white underwear and blue jeans for all of us, rather than one of my usual carefully sorted loads of whites, darks, or colors.

I get a big sirloin steak out of the freezer. The broiler on the old stove died a year and a half ago and I promised the family that the first meal on a new stove would be steak.

At lunch, Bob and I talk about the threat some more. We speculate on where we would go if we were to evacuate. We list all the relatives: my brothers in Rhode Island, Virginia and North Carolina, his brother in Cleveland, our married daughter in New Hampshire and our other daughter at New York University. "We can't worry about Becky (at N.Y.U.)," Bob says. "She's on her own and probably will be okay. The main reason to leave would be to protect the kids at home." None of the authorities has mentioned any specific danger to adolescents but I feel a concern for the ripening gonads in our house.

After lunch, I opt for a nap. My metabolism has been doing double time and I am really tired. Bob and Ann settle down at the dining room table for a tutoring session in algebra. Ann admits that she is nine lessons behind. I can almost hear Bob's inward groan as I head upstairs.

After my nap, I feel better, not nearly so anxious and more optimistic about the outcome of this modern-day crisis. It is a nice afternoon and I hang some of the laundry outdoors. I had recently decided that if the labor that a labor-saving device saved me was active labor, I would spurn the device and do the labor. How ridiculous to grow   flabby pushing buttons and then to do hateful exercises to tone up your muscles.

I come in and vacuum the rug in the front hall. I am buying an Oriental rug from a friend who sells them. I have six home on approval and it's time to put another one down so we can see how we like it. I roll up the Ardebil and roll out a Yalemeh.

In the late afternoon, Adam comes home. "Boy," he says, "what a mess downtown. It took me half an hour to get off I-95 at Delaware Avenue this morning because of lane restrictions on Brandywine Bridge."

"My God," says Bob, "not another bridge! How many does that make?"

For some time traffic in and out of Wilmington has been in a tangle because of a sudden closing of a main bridge over the Brandywine River, which divides the city roughly into one-third and two-third sections where it passes through. The Augustine bridge was closed over a year ago after a team of inspectors pronounced it unsafe. It was threatening to fall of its own weight and not even pedestrians have been allowed on it. There were several results. One was a concern for and inspection of

all the remaining bridges over both the Brandywine River and the Chris-
tina, at the southern boundary of the city. Another was increased traffic
on smaller bridges which weren't meant to carry the load. The added
burden of two severe winters caused the surfaces of the lesser bridges to
become an obstacle course of pot-holes. And the inspection turned up
other deteriorating bridges.

We go for the paper again. Road closings due to repairs are listed on
Saturdays for the coming week. These are the bridges on the list:
Third Street Bridge—detours in effect through September for con-
struction of a new bridge

Augustine Bridge—closed indefinitely, unsafe structure

Rising Sun Road Bridge—closed through June 11 for reconstruction

Brandywine Bridge on I-95—lane restrictions in both directions
through April for bridge approach slab replacement

There were further lane restrictions on I-95 because they are widen-
ing a viaduct just south of the city.

Was Bob thinking what I was? Suppose there is an emergency involv-
ing Wilmington? How will anyone get out when there are only a few
routes open? It makes me want to put everyone in the car right then
and take off. But like the Jews in Hitler's Europe, I think of reasons
why I can't: We've waited so long for that nice steak dinner; Ann has a
piano recital tomorrow and she can't miss that. Besides, I haven't finished the laundry. And what about Jane's rugs? Can I just leave them here?
I am not ready to leave and I don't even know where to go.

We have our steak dinner and spend the evening reading and watching tv. None of the regular programs is pre-empted. I finish folding the
laundry before I go to bed.

Meeting for Worship is at 9:15 on Sunday mornings. Bob and I go
regularly. The children came with us when they were younger but now
find it too boring. The Sunday paper has not been delivered by the time
we must leave. All the local radio stations run religious programs on Sunday mornings so we do not turn on the radio for news.

On the ride to Friends School, where our meetings are held, I wonder
if Meeting will be about the nuclear crisis. I hope it won't. I am enjoying
a period of relative inner calm because of my temporary ignorance of
the latest developments.

Our meeting is very small, only twenty-nine adult members and
about as many children. There are also some regular attenders. Jan is
one. Margaret is a newly-joined member. They are not here today. We
settle into the wonderful silence. The first person to speak is a young
man who shares all his worries—about failing courses and changing jobs
and unpaid bills. The following speakers address themselves to how to

deal with one's own feelings of inadequacy. Nothing about Three Mile Island.

Nonetheless, I spend a portion of the meeting picking a place to go. I decide that Cleveland is the place, well west of the prevailing winds.

When we get home, the Sunday paper is there with an ominous headline: MASS EVACUATION POSSIBLE, U.S. SAYS. The lead article says federal officials were calling the bubble inside the crippled reactor "potentially explosive" but disagreed on how soon that might be a problem. One official said twelve days, another said only two. At an earlier news conference: "NRC Chairman Joseph M. Hendrie said that evacuation of citizens within ten to twenty miles downwind of the power plant was 'certainly a possibility' as a precaution if technicians tried to force the bubble out of the reactor."

The article goes on to explain the dangers of removing the bubble. One way, reducing the pressure in the reactor, might cause the bubble to expand too much and expose the fuel rods, allowing them to overheat. Blowing out the water and the bubble by a sudden release of pressure followed by instant injections of new cooling water "might risk damaging the fuel with violent pressure changes." A third way would be to continue circulating cooling water normally, letting it "slowly sweep away the gas bubble, bit by bit." The danger in this method is that it could take too long and the bubble might become explosive before it was removed.

The bubble is filled with hydrogen. It is slowly mixing with oxygen. The mixture will be explosive if the proportion of oxygen gets high enough. Therefore, *not* removing the bubble is also hazardous.

I notice another article. A reporter has interviewed people coming out of the theater where "The China Syndrome," a movie about a meltdown, is playing. It just came to town this week. I don't want to read anymore. Why would anyone want to see such a movie this weekend?

We eat lunch and I go up to my room to read my current book. I tell Ann to call me at two-thirty. Her recital is at three-thirty.

At 2:45 she and I are driving down I-95. At the Brandywine bridge we are squeezed over onto the shoulder and a portion of the Delaware Avenue exit ramp. Farther south, on the viaduct, we are again squeezed to the right. There is not much traffic. We are never stopped, only slowed to thirty-five miles per hour. But wait until tomorrow. What a mess this will all be then with weekday traffic and all the construction men and machines in operation.

When we arrive at the music building of the university, we take seats in the small auditorium. Ann will sit with me until her performance is announced. I like recitals. I get a big kick out of observing the kids. Some are so earnest and concentrate so hard on the mechanics of their pieces, playing perfectly, completely without style. Others are the embodiment of insouciance, even if they make mistakes. When her turn comes, I can see that Ann is trying to cover up her nervousness. She plays her two pieces quite well even though she makes a couple of mistakes. Actually, I marvel at how good she is and at how long (six years) she has stuck with her piano lessons. And for what?

Having children is based on the assumption that civilization will continue and that it is worthwhile to transmit the cultural and ethical values one lives by. But today I am uncertain about both of these assumptions. I have not taught Ann how to *survive*, and that's what she needs to know. I wonder again, as I have so many times lately, if women had been in charge of making the life and death decisions (in this case, of whether to pursue nuclear power) would the results be the same?

The recital ends and we file out. Ann accepts praise from her piano teacher who is obviously pleased with her pupil.

We drive back up I-95, through the northbound constriction, and home.

On the five-thirty news there are shots of President and Mrs. Carter inspecting the Three Mile Island plant—a move obviously designed to reassure us.

I make dinner and we all eat. After dinner, I read more of the Sunday paper. I pick up on an article about Delaware's civil defense plan. It proves Jan right. "The plan says an airborne release of radioactive material allows little time for reaction. During the initial period—four to five hours—speedy action is critical in avoiding undue exposure."

The first warning will be a steady siren blast of three to five minutes. "If weather or other conditions preclude evacuation, the public would be asked to stay inside, shut windows and turn off ventilation to keep outside air from entering homes and buildings."

There are certainly conditions which preclude evacuation. There is no gasoline, there is an airline strike, and the highway system is a jumble of closed bridges and construction and lane restrictions. And even I am enough of a physicist to know that staying inside is not much protection against radioactive fallout.

Later, Adam and I watch the regular Sunday programs on tv while Bob and Ann work some more on Ann's algebra. At ten o'clock, everyone but me goes to bed. I wait up for the eleven o'clock news, still trying to make some decision about what to do.

On the news, the President mentions the possible evacuation of people within a ten mile radius of the plant. "If it becomes necessary, Governor Thornburgh will ask you to take appropriate action. If he does, I want the instructions to be carried out as calmly as they have been in the past few days."

That does it. I shut off the set and head for bed, my mind whirling. I know what I am going to do. If the order comes to evacuate that ten-mile radius, we go, too. The officials don't seem to know what will happen if they tinker with that bubble and I'm not going to wait for them to be certain. Tomorrow I will get ready.

When I get up Monday morning, I am journey-proud. The list of things I must do drums in my head. Adam eats his breakfast and tears out to catch his ride to high school. Bob and I have a few minutes alone at the breakfast table before he must leave for work.

"I've decided what I'm going to do," I tell him.

"Oh, really," he says, "what have you decided?"

"If they evacuate the ten-mile radius around the plant, I'm going too."

"Where are you going to go?," he asks.

"To David's" (his brother in Cleveland), I say. "And I'm going to offer to pick up your mother and father on the way."

Bob's parents live north of here near Allentown, Pennsylvania, roughly in the same radius from Harrisburg as Wilmington. They are in their seventies and no longer drive long distance.

"What a nice idea," Bob says. "Can I come too?"

I laugh. It feels so good. I don't think I've laughed all weekend. "Of course, you dummy," I say.

Ann comes into the diningroom, her beautiful blond hair freshly blown dry and shimmering. We stop talking about my plan and each gives Ann a little pep talk about her upcoming algebra test.

She groans.

We all finish our breakfasts. Bob and Ann leave. I pour another cup of coffee and read the morning paper. There is a front-page picture of President Carter wearing plastic booties as he tours the crippled nuclear plant. At the bottom of the page another article grabs my attention. TRUCKING INDUSTRY ANNOUNCES NAT'L TEAMSTERS LOCKOUT, says the headline. The Teamsters called a selective strike against seventy-five companies over the weekend. However, Trucking Management, Inc., the trucking industries' bargaining group "refused to participate in the divide-and-conquer strategy." In its statement it said it "had no alternative but to instruct its member associations and authorizing carriers to shut down their operations in defense against the strike. This will cause a major disruption in trucking transportation—not a limited selective stoppage."

Local business men indicated that a Teamsters strike could cause perishable goods to be in short supply by the coming weekend.

"The Interstate Commerce Commission said yesterday there was an 'urgent and immediate' need for alternative sources of transportation."

I close the paper and clean up breakfast, making plans as I do. Now, with a Teamsters strike upon us, I decide I must buy food. Not only is there a chance that our food supply will be contaminated, it may not even be delivered to the stores. How fragile we have made our civilization. As an individual, I have no idea whether I will be able to survive the ultimate nuclear disaster. I do know that the dividing line is crossed. The risks I take now will be the cautious/foolish ones, not the heedless/foolish.

I take a shower and make mental notes on what clothing we should take—jeans, shirts and warm jackets. I think about the photographs. In case of a fire, I have always planned to try to rescue the photographs because they are irreplaceable. How about if they are irradiated? Should I pack the photographs? I simply cannot handle the thoughts of a totally uncertain future. I will get us through a week of chaos. That's as much as I can manage.

As I am making a list of things to do, the phone rings. It's Bob.

"Don't go to the bank," he says. "I just emptied our accounts."

"You did?"

"Yes...I figured if there was an emergency, what we'd need is cash. And if we wait until it happens, we won't have time to get it."

I hadn't thought about money. I'm grateful Bob is assuming some responsibility. "How much did you get?" I ask.

"One thousand in cash and four thousand in traveler's checks."

"Holy smoke," I say, "I didn't know we had that much. I hope there's still fifty dollars left for me to get some groceries."

"I just got paid on Friday," he says, "and I didn't take the checking account down to zero, so it ought to be ok to cash fifty dollars. One of the guys here is all ready. His car is packed with camping gear and he's ready to pull out on a minute's notice."

"Well, that's what I decided," I say. "I'm going to fill the gas tank and buy a week's worth of canned foods and just leave them in the trunk of the car. When you come home tonight, we'll call David and your parents."

I tell him about the Teamsters' strike and we hang up. I can't believe I'm doing this. I think about Bob's being seven miles away when he is at work. Would he have time to get home? At least his job is on the same side of the river as our house, so he doesn't have to worry about how to get across it. And to go to his parents we would head north. The kids' schools are both within a mile of home so I know I could collect them.

When I get to the discount grocery, which sells only non-perishable goods, I hedge my bets. I buy everything I can in a liquid state in case the water supply is contaminated or interrupted. But I also buy a twenty-quart box of powdered milk in case it's not. Some of the things I buy, such as canned Vienna sausages, are strictly emergency rations. We would never eat them unless we had to. I buy lots of canned juices and evaporated milk so we will have enough to drink. Canned beans, tuna fish, chicken chow mein, chili and canned fruits. At the checkout counter I spot packages of flashlight batteries and buy two. I remember reading a story years ago about a nuclear attack. The people in the story had food but no soap and no toilet paper. I pay for the stuff and pack it into the bags I've brought with me.

Now I feel a strong need to talk to someone. All weekend I have felt isolated in my own thoughts and fears. I need to see what other people are doing. I decide to go to the Elementary Workshop. The Elementary Workshop is a private, parent-cooperative school that Ann and Adam attended. Some of the people who work there became my best friends. I can usually find someone who will stop for a quick cup of coffee.

The Workshop is housed in an unused Catholic school in a section of Wilmington that was razed for slum clearance fifteen years ago. The front door is kept locked to reduce the pilferage and vandalism. When I ring the bell, Jana answers. Her mother, Carolyn, works at the school and is one of my friends. Jana goes to public school.

"Hi, Jana!" I say. "What are you doing here?"

"My mom wouldn't let me go to school today," Jana says. "She wants me here in case we have to leave town because of that Three Mile Island stuff."

"Wow," I say, "a free holiday."

But Jana grumbles. "I really wanted to go to school today. We were going to dissect a frog in science class."

Wilmington schools were desegregated this year. Jana lives in the city but she is bused to a junior high school in the county. It is a forty minute ride.

I go into the office. Carolyn is there. I tell her I've just come from buying my week's supply of emergency rations.

"I'm all packed," Carolyn says. "The car is all loaded with camping gear and food. I figure when the siren blows we have four or five hours and I plan to be the first one out."

Carolyn is divorced. Her son, Rusty, attends the Workshop. She is keeping everyone together today. I'm reassured. I talk to Carolyn for a while and leave.

I fill up the gas tank on the way home. When Bob comes home we will decide together whether to put the camping gear in the trunk. We must also arrange a meeting place in case he's at work when we decide to leave.

As I eat lunch I realize how much more relaxed I am. I have a plan; I know what I am going to do. If the word comes to evacuate Harrisburg, I'll grab some clothes for each of us, fill three or four water jugs, pick up the kids, meet Bob—and we're off.

After lunch, I make two or three calls about the old stove, and find a company that will pick it up for two dollars and arrange for them to come. Then I go upstairs for my afternoon read.

When the kids come home, I tell them about my plan. Ann says it's a good idea. Adam says he thinks it's dumb. They turn on the tv to watch the rerun of "M.A.S.H." at 3:30. When the program ends, the four o'clock newsbreak announcer says the hydrogen bubble in the reactor has shrunk to a much safer size. There is less threat of its replacing the reactor's cooling water.

"See," Adam says, "I told you it was dumb."

Right, I think. I hope you're right.

Bob brings home an evening paper. It says the critical time for a possible explosion from a chemical reaction within the reactor "has moved out considerable" from the five days predicted yesterday by Harold Denton of the NRC.

So we don't call David and we don't pack the camping gear. By the next morning, Tuesday, April third, the situation looks quite hopeful. During the day the announcement comes that "we no longer consider a hydrogen explosion a significant problem."

I leave the food in the car for another week. On Tuesday, April tenth, *The Morning News* says the "crisis is over." Governor Thornburgh says it is safe for preschool children and pregnant women to return to their homes within five miles of the Three Mile Island plant. Bob deposits our cash the following day. In the meantime, I buy a rug and enjoy a delayed elation over my wonderful new stove.

The Sunday paper for April twenty-ninth has a small article about the reactor. The temperature in the reactor has fallen below boiling for the first time since the accident.

The next morning Bob cashes in the traveler's checks with the same woman who sold them to him. She remembers him. "Didn't you go on your trip?" she asks.

"No," says Bob, "it just didn't work out."

Robert Stewart
EVACUATION PLAN

It's as though we were being asked
simply to leave old hatreds

to gather everyone we love
and to be sure the raw meat is fresh

which we carry through the aftermath.
Proverbs become nourishing

as freeze-dried stroganoff or any
old spiritual values, double-dug

in the forest loam of salvation:
food we buy today, we eat tomorrow.

*

Seventy years ago the tightest ship
ever built came to a halt

in the icy sea; men lowered
their families as if into grace.

"Watch out for the suction,"
their final instructions to the world.

Soon the only sound in a concentric
circle of small boats

was oars stroking hard to pull away.
In the morning ice was everywhere.

*

It's as though we were being asked
to drift: from the crest of the Andes

to the Amazon where life, unaccounted,
creeps through millenia.

There are so many similes for peace.
I tell my son that "host areas" really exist

and take him with me to the edge—
some county line we have been crossing

like hybrids or tropical air plants
settling into that unknown soil

where each species clings
to its ration of raw meat and hope.

Eugene McCarthy
ETERNAL REVENUE SERVICE

AN AXIOM of long standing is that "nothing is more certain than death and taxes." At the same time, whereas it is generally held that there is life after death, it has also been held that once an estate was settled, there would be no more taxes after death.

So taxpayers who looked forward or upward to the relief from taxes as one of the joys of the hereafter must have been deeply disillusioned by a recent announcement from the Treasury Department.

In anticipation of a nuclear attack and the destruction, confusion and near chaos that might follow, a senior Treasury official has prepared a plan "for collecting taxes even under those difficult conditions." Even annihilation does not bring escape from the Internal Revenue Service.

The plan is called "A Design of an Emergency Tax System." The "design's" first concern is to perpetuate the Individual Income Tax system by securing the records on the basis of which taxes are determined. Taxes owed by those who are annihilated will be assessed as best they can be, the report states.

It would be a convenience to the IRS if the nuclear attack could be coordinated with the April 15 deadline (no pun intended) for income-tax payments. If that date is not possible, perhaps the powers that be could manage it on or soon after one of the days on which quarterly payments of estimated taxes are scheduled.

The Treasury design does not make public its plans for the safety and survival of IRS agents. Possibly the agents may be lost, but in the short run—for five or six months after the attack—the computers, in some safe place, will continue the essential work of the IRS.

The design notes that nuclear war might be so disastrous that, in addition to the destruction of millions of people, major industrial installations and major population centers, it might even destroy the tax system. This, the IRS seems to believe, would be the most serious consequence of nuclear war. There are some experts in post-nuclear-war survival who hold that, along with cockroaches, the income-tax system is likely to be among the few survivors of such war.

Taking no chances, however, the author of the design proposes a standby tax program in the form of a general sales tax to be applied at the point of purchase.

Such a tax, the author holds, would have two advantages: It would encourage savings and "aid in rebuilding the capital stock" of the country.

The Treasury expert has even set the percentage level for the tax: 20 percent. He says this should do it. That does not quite square with the Mutual Assured Destruction concept, developed by Robert McNamara as Secretary of Defense, which held that deterrence would occur at the prospect of the loss of 20 percent of the population and 50 percent of industrial capacity.

The design does not make clear who will collect the tax or whether it will be applied to the costs of mortician services, although in the immediate post-bombing period, such goods and services would make up a major part of the gross national product.

The danger with a plan of this kind, a contingency plan, is not in its being there in anticipation of the emergency for which it was drafted. It is probably as good a plan as any that could be devised for conditions that no one can anticipate.

The danger lies in the fact that Treasury and the IRS may become attached to the plan to the point that without the nuclear war for which it was prepared, they may come to believe that the plan offers a better tax system than the one currently in place. They might offer it as a substitute, with the sustaining argument that, apart from the merits of their tax program, it would be a good idea to have the emergency program established in advance of the emergency.

A contingency plan can be a destabilizing force, as those who conceived it may become more and more attached to it, and eager to test it, with or without an emergency.

The attempted takeover of a military government in Greece a few years ago by another military group is a recent example. The attempt was based on a contingency plan to take over the government if it were communist-controlled—which this one was not.

The lesson is to beware of bureaucrats (or generals) bearing contingency plans. Possibly, under bureaucracy, you not only cannot take it with you, but you cannot even leave it behind.

Hillel Schwartz
GALATEA'S NEWSSTAND

Without duplication
there could be no wars;
anger and envy may be original
but wars need records,
thumbprints, ways to know
your friends. I started
in the Great War,
selling carbon paper
to the neutral Swiss,
who kept the files
for both sides.
I learned that war
is an act of copying:
uniforms, espionage,
propaganda. Propaganda.
Everything has to happen
twice: words, people
must be redundant.
I stood in the middle
of offices, watching
the new typewriters
pound like mortars,
my carbons echoing
through to the end.
When the war died
for lack of ribbons,
I left Europe for Cincinnati,
married and opened
a salon, twenty mirrors
and all the chemicals
to reproduce faces
in modern magazines.
Now I am an old woman
back in the paper trade.
My children have children
and none of them looks

like me. I have left
my husband and want
a faithful lover, a man
to illustrate my stories,
a man to dance them,
uncompromising as the wars
that drove them into my skin
like the memories of Hiroshima
planted in shadow on the bodies
of the accurate replica dead.

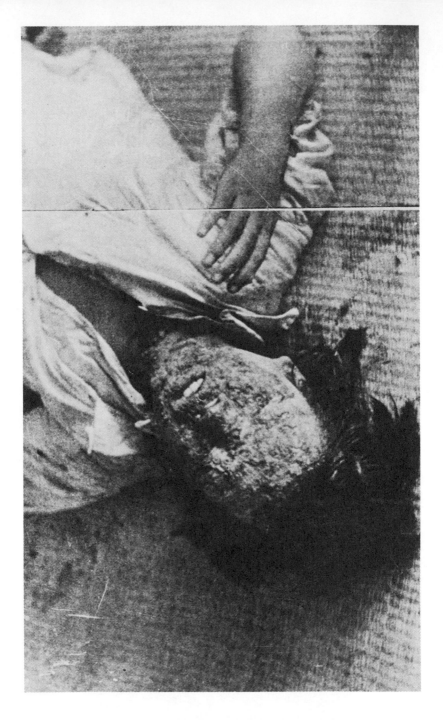

Anonymous / photo
provided by the 1962 Mayor of Hiroshima & Curt Johnson

W.D. Ehrhart
SUNSET

Dresden Nuclear Power Station, Morris, Illinois

Late afternoon: in the stillness
before evening, a car on the road
between cornfields surrounding
Dresden Station raises a plume
of dust, and a light wind
settles the dust gently over the corn.
Power lines over the cornfields
audibly sing the power of cities
beyond sight, where neon lights flash
tomorrow, laughter and dreams.
Deep within Dresden Station,
human beings tamper with atoms.

Dresden: say it, and the air
fills with the wail of sirens,
thin fingers of light
frantically probing the clouds,
red bursting anger, black thunder,
the steel drone of the heavy bombers,
dry bones rattle of falling bombs:
    deliver us from fire;
    deliver us from the flames;
    Lord, have mercy upon us.
135,000 human beings
died in the flames of Dresden.

The air to the west is on fire.
The lake to the west burns red
with the sun's descending fire.
The sky rises out of the lake gold
to copper to deep blue, falling
gently away, black, to the east.
Deep within Dresden Station,
human beings tamper with atoms.

contd.

Light wind rustles the cornstalks,
the sound like the rustle of skirts
on young graceful women.

Rolf Jacobsen
GREEN LIGHT

Creatures that rustle in the shadows, all the crooked
deformed ones in the world, with tiny feet and far too many eyes,
can hide in the grass—that's why it's there,
silent and full of moonlight among the continents.

I have lived in the grass among the small ones who resemble
        broken twigs.
From their towers of cowslip the bumblebees came like bells
into my heart with words of a magic species.
The winds took my poem and spread it out like dust.

I have lived in the grass with the Earth and I have heard it breathe
like an animal that has walked a long way and is thirsting for the
        waterholes,
and I felt it lie down heavily on its side in the evening like a
        buffalo,
in the darkness between the stars, where there is room.

The dance of the winds and the great wildfires in the grass I
        remember often:
—The silhouetted smiles of a face that always shows forgiveness.
But why it has such great patience with us
deep down in its iron brain, its huge magnesium heart, we are far
        from understanding.

For we have forgotten this: that the Earth is a star of grass,
a seed-planet, swirling with spores as with clouds, from sea to sea,
a whirl of them. Seeds take hold under the cobblestones
and between the letters in my poem, here they are.

Don Dolan / pen & ink

Jascha Kessler
TEIRESIAS

SATURDAY MORNING we decided to travel all the way downtown for a change. It was one of those memorable days when March has just blown itself out and April has not yet warmed and gathered its damp tinctures of sulfuric smuts. We were after nothing really but a view of the fast-flowing waters of the Bay, of the Statue of Liberty, and the great bridges arching East and West, and the shapeless forest of gray hulls and masts over in Brooklyn, like the dead trees in a great swamp. No one is crowded then in the shadowed canyons of the financial district: on Saturday morning the overreaching walls of stones and glass refract clouds and the sky in harsh cubistic angles. Only strollers, shoppers for oddments, traverse the narrow streets, thinking of hardware, exotic lumber, surplus paper, sundries, electronic gear and salvage. The offices are silent, dark, rank upon rank above the old winding abyssal streets. Alpha to Omega: the first Dutch cowpaths and village tracks, now paved over yet persistent beneath asphalt, enduring the unimaginable, mortgaged future entailed in the skyscrapers. Only a very deep, frozen granite plug into the magma beneath the mantle of Terra could sustain the weight piled up on Manhattan Island down there near the Battery. One feels lighter, smaller than an ant in that district. But on such a Saturday morning, noontime, springtime, one's soul caroms about those breezy canyons, free for an hour from the corridors of work in our pharaonic temples.

Up Nassau we wandered after circling the tip from Wall and out along the railing over the sparkling, tangy Bay waters. We looked into old stores, with their high ceilings and carved oaken lintels. Now and then, to the East and the North, a glimpse of the high decks of the Brooklyn Bridge swaying quaint and stolid up there over the East River. We stopped somewhere at the end of Nassau Street before a dusty store window. The building must have been a chandler's warehouse in the 1800s, judging from the anchors crossed over the first story. Most of it seemed derelict now, boarded up. But the door was open. Let's go in, I said.

Such an array of ill-sorted junk: hardware, war-surplus equipment and clothing, canteens, webbed belts, boots, tents, mess kits and rubberized ponchos, rusted machetes and trenching tools, all laid out on rickety tables and stacked up on metal shelving, up to the high ceiling where weak bulbs dangled from naked cords. Anything can be found in a store like that. Sometimes the quality is fine: reams of 25-pound rag paper, big old ledgers with creamy stock, wide margins, deckled edges and leather binding. I saw a display case stacked with cigar boxes, and asked the proprietor, who had come out now and stood there in baggy striped pants, a ravelled, wool cardigan of faded scarlet and silver, white-haired, pinkfaced and smoothshaven and smoking a fine meerschaum on whose bowl a mer-

maid swam forward like a Naiad on the bowsprit of a clipper, I asked
him if by some chance he had any vintage Habanas tucked away there?
You never know. "No, nothing like that," he said, puffing away rather
contemptuously, I thought, even sneeringly. Well, what was in those fine
Monte Cristo boxes? He reached down and handed me one: instead of
Churchill Corona Coronas, it held shiny clips of neat copper and brass
fingers, oiled 7.65 ammo. I see, I said. "So you do," he replied, taking
the box and placing it back carefully with the others stacked up in the
case. Would you perhaps have a good shotgun for me? "If you like, I
might have something for you, yes." He turned towards the partition
that divided the store. My wife frowned at me, but followed after.

We went round to the rear of the store. This part was much cleaner
than the front: the floor waxed, the cabinets highly-polished oak and
walnut, their glass clear. In the middle of the floor stood a pair of .50
caliber machine guns on tripods, World War I types. They looked ready
for use, belts of rounds draped out and folded in their metal boxes like
metallic tripes. There were bazookas on fine old mahogany tables; there
were grenade launchers, recoilless rocket guns, 200mm mortars, automatic cannons, a Bofors anti-aircraft gun. In the cases pistols of all sizes,
and rifles in the cabinets, Brownings, Mausers, Mannlichers, M-1s, M-16s.
My wife picked up a Kalashnikov assault rifle and hefted it. I turned the
wavering muzzle away and said she ought to keep her finger off the trigger. "This is more like it," she said, cradling it under the crook of her
arm like a guerilla and sweeping in a circle. I said she should keep her fingers out of the trigger guard.

The proprietor stood up from behind the large case then. He'd been
stooped over and fussing in a low drawer. He smiled wanly at me around
the ember mouthpiece of his pipe as he held out a large gun. "This is
what I think you might be wanting, I think. Something extraordinary."
I took it from him. It was an old shotgun, a make I didn't recognize. It
was quite beautiful, and I said so. The stock was burl walnut; the breech
of heavy silver, engraved all over with a forest of flowers and curvetting
stags and leaping hounds; the barrels were blued to perfection, satiny,
oiled; the trigger guard gilded and velvety to the touch. Perfectly bal-
anced: it went up against my shoulder as though made for me. It broke
apart at a touch: the action was almost liquid. "Traps, hunting, whatever you like with a weapon like this," he said, puffing away. I turned it
about, just to enjoy the feel of it, and noticed a silver plate sunk in the
heel of the stock. It had letters engraved in elaborated Gothic script.
When I made them out I was surprised: entwined with minute patterns
of stylized small game and oak leaves, the name was mine. What a coincidence! I said.

The proprietor, who was watching my wife toying with the deadly,
Russian automatic weapon, raised his eyebrows shaggily, but said nothing. Neither did he move to warn her himself or take it from her, though
it made me uneasy, her behaving that way behind my back. She hated

guns, so I thought she was being sardonic. I wanted her to look at this
shotgun of mine. It's quite a coincidence! I said again. "I don't know,"
the proprietor finally replied, still watching her, "but we could find out,
couldn't we." I only wish we could, I said.

He hauled out a great old record book then, dropped it down on the
counter top, and began thumbing through it. It was like the registers you
still see sometimes in some decrepit spa in Europe somewhere, full of
names and numbers written in every kind of hand, splotched here and
there, and glowing in the faded inks of all the colors of the rainbow.
How old was that book? I wondered. The proprietor was in no hurry.
He seemed to relish the chance to browse through it while I waited: I
could see the pleasure he took in it, as though running over the pedigrees
of fine old guns of the last two centuries reminded him of the very weapons themselves. That must be a rare catalogue, I said. All yours? "So it
is," he said. "So they were." The paper was a heavy, ribbed parchment;
the early signatures were almost faded out or illegible with weevil holes.
The latter third of the volume was, however, still unused, and the paper
fresh as though it had been bound yesterday. Seems up to date, doesn't
it. "Yes," he mumbled, running his arthritic and tobacco-stained finger
down a column, the nails of that gnarled hand broken and black with
dottle—he had a way of tamping the hot wad in his meerschaum down as
though he couldn't even feel the fire of the glowing ember he puffed at.
"Here we are," he said in a voice that showed no happiness in having
found the record of this gun. A neutral voice, bored in fact. "There are
only two others like it. This one has had but three owners since it was
made ... oh, about 1928 or 1929, I should imagine." Where does it
come from? "It's a German make. Can't you see that?" He was sneering
at me. I suppose so. Well, how did it get to America then? and how did
it come to you, I said. I was almost shouting at him. Well?

He shrugged at me. He wasn't telling. He pointed at the names in the
ledger again. I couldn't read them upside down, and all I could make out
was that it had been sold three times. After the War, the space went
blank. I'll buy it, of course. I had decided right there. "But can you afford an item like this after all?" he said, not to me but to my wife, as
though she were the one to ask. I turned and held it out to her. Whatever
it costs, I said, we're buying it. She tucked the light and dangerous Kalashnikov weapon under her arm again and stood there, legs apart, looking sceptically at me and my shotgun. I admitted the price seemed rather
high. But, I said, the name on it was mine, too. And so .... "And so?"
she said. That was my reason, I said. She demurred, "Strange, yes, but—"
But nothing! The point is, Who's that original owner! How did he come
to have my name!

She wasn't listening. The proprietor had stepped round me. He was
putting the leather strap of that Kalashnikov over her shoulder. He was
showing her how to release the safety catch. She followed his bony fingers with her long, soft ones. My own voice sounded dim in my ears, so
long ago, and faraway.

D. Nurkse
LAMPS AND FENCES

When the dead came into power
at first we did not notice

the stars were a little brighter
there were more roaches
wherever we walked
we killed something

since it was involuntary
it happened as if in secret

in the bars the prices
were written in chalk

the musicians were too eager to finish
though they remained true
to the old rage

When we made love
our thoughts turned to the hunted

and those turned back
from the frontier

Though the frontier was only
the meaning of a sound
in a language that had mastered us

CLOSED BORDERS

The State draws a line
between my death and my father's.

He fell and was buried,
the shovel forgot him,
I forgot him.

But I take my place
in a line of travelers,
each with a suitcase
containing a damp toothbrush
and spare clothes.

There's no more past
to claim us.
We're going to the State.

On the way, we keep asking
the fire for death, as if
the fire had one last secret.

Marge Piercy
THE TRACK OF THE MASTER BUILDER

Pyramids of flesh sweated pyramids of stone
as slaves chiseled their stolen lives in rock
over the gilded chrysalis of dead royal grub.
The Romans built roads for marching armies
hacked like swords straight to the horizon.
Gothic cathedrals: a heaven of winter clouds
crystallizing as they rained into stone caves,
choirs of polyphonic light striking chilly slabs
where nobles with swords on and skinny saints
lay under the floor.
                              Fortresses, dungeons, keeps,
moats and bulwarks. Palaces with mirrored halls;
rooms whose views unfold into each other
like formal gardens, offer vistas and symmetry.
Skyscrapers where nobody lives filled with paper.

Where do the people live and what have they made themselves
splendid as these towers of glass, these groves of stone?
The impulse that in 1910 cast banks as temples,
where now does it build its numinous artiface?
The ziggurat, the acropolis, the palace of our dream
whose shape rings in the blood's cave like belladonna,
take form in the eagle's preyseeking soar
of the bomber, those planes expensive as cities,
the shark lean submarines of nuclear death,
the taut kinetic tower of the missile,
the dark fiery omphalos of the all-killing bomb.

William Pitt Root

THE DAY THE SUN RISES TWICE

The day the sun rises twice
the primitive dream of fire comes true,
fire that burns forever.,
fire no water on earth can quench,
fire whose light pins shadows to the stones,
fire whose killing edge turns flying birds to ash.

Aeons after the last of the one-eyed prophets
has chanted into that permanent darkness
no archeologist shall unearth,
countless minute embers will linger among the omens.

I make this black mark on the silence now
because none shall write
and none shall remain to read
when the clouds rise in our eyes
against those suns rising around us
like the thousand trees of life all clad in flames.

Robert Creeley

ON SAUL BELLOW'S THESIS, THAT WE THINK
OUR ERA'S AWFUL BECAUSE WE'LL DIE IN IT

Not only that you're going to die in it,
but that it will kill you! There is

no way you'll get out of it, away from it,
alive. Neither money nor hope

nor any other damn thing will make the least difference.
And there won't even be a you left

to contest this most meager provision,
your life. You think that's bad?

Isn't this your life and aren't
you the one presumably who's living it?

Jacques Prevert
THE DUNCE

He says no with his head
but yes with his heart
he says yes to what he loves
he says no to the teacher
he is standing
he is questioned
and all the problems are posed
suddenly his crazy laugh takes him
and he erases everything
the figures and the words
the dates and the names
the phrases and the snares
and in spite of the master's threats
under the hoots of child prodigies
with chalk of every color
on the blackboard of misfortune
he draws the face of happiness.

—translated by Chael Graham

Will Inman
6 AUGUST 1981

36 years later
and how many days before

oh, say can you see

>>> he sewed it on the
>>> seat of his blue jeans

>> Enola Gay donated by
>> Harry Truman

by dawn's early light

>>> a cop dragged his ass
>>> till the flag came loose

>> to hang in the main hall
>> of the United Nations Assembly

what so proudly we

>>> charged him with indecent
>>> exposure

>> plastered all over with
>> 200,000 decals of rising
>> suns

in the twilight's last

>>> —flag was raised, so to
>>> speak, there he was, he
>>> always got excited by rough
>>> treatment

o'er the ramparts we
watched

>>> so they gave him time
>>> in the city jail tank

>> of course Truman never
>> really

>>> passed him around in the
>>> tank   like a joint

>> still all those people—
>> Oppenheimer said his hands

so gallantly streaming

                                    his speech and everything
else about him was free, all
right—to everybody *else*
in that jail tank

                  were bloody
and the rockets red

                  Truman called Oppenheimer
                  a cry baby
                                when he got out, went on a
bombs bursting in
            those tears were fall-out
                                rampage, burnt every flag he
                                could get his hands on, he
              eating all our descendants'
proof through the night
that our flag was
                                arrested again and put in the
            bone marrow

o say does that star
                                this time sentenced to
                                prison for destruction of
                                public
                  proof to the Russians we would
yet wave
                                a model prisoner
              do anything
o'er the land of the
                                free to choose a more
                                practical response
              to keep our
home of the
                                brave public opinion
                                and peer pressure alike
                                to start life over
                                with the American flag not
                                in the seat of his

my

            country

                              jeans, though from now on
                              he would publicly dress
                              more suitably

'tis of thee

            so i believe, Mr Chairman
            we should really donate
            to the United Nations

sweet land of liberty

                              and be a proper citizen
            the historic airplane
            Enola Gay
of thee i

                              singled out for his
                              conversion while behind bars
           as a reminder to the peoples
           of the world
land where our fathers

                              tried to spread the Word
           how terrible
land of the pilgrims'

                              pride in his new existence
           the Bomb can be
from every mountain

                              one side has to be right
           so we must all
let freedom

                              don't you ring me, i'll
                              ring you: you see, he has
                              learned how to
           avoid confusion

o beautiful for spacious

                              moved to the Sun Belt
                              where he set up a business
           and present our
waves of grain

                              to the highest bidder
              American Way
above the fruited
                              plainly is more practical and
              the best way
God shed his grace on
                              a fresh start for everyone
              with a tax cut
confirm thy
                              goods for everyone with a
                              dollar
              let them have the Enola Gay
              and we can withdraw from You Enn
              and go back to clean
              heterosexual
with liberty
              and justice
                              will trickle down to
the Halls of Montezuma
              that's enough of that
                              like oil from
the shores of Tripoli

              enough!
                              uh-oh, now he's arrested for
                              tax evasion
We Interrupt The Music To
Bring You This News Bulletin:
Today An Unknown Soldier
Has Dropped The First
                              his lawyer stated from now on
                              he will make no statements
since Hiroshima and Nagasaki
              following the news we always
              bring you good news
              from God's Word
                              possible sentence of
no word from the blasted area
no flights over the fall-out

1st Corinthians:
Speak ecstasy to God, speak
prophecy to humankind: prophecy
can build, can stimulate, can
bring hope to the people
                    five years and a fine of
radioactivity for how long can

        build community among those of
        good
                    may seem excessive but
no choice but to start

6, 8 August 1981

Hank De Leo / pen & ink

Hugh Fox
from VOICES

What *was*,
In the days of the great thought cable,
In the days of the solar satellite birds,
In the days of the moving screen games,
They shall never come again in the depths of our affliction,
The spear-towers that goaded the stars,
The destruction of the race of hairy giants,
The machines of wheat,
The machines of corn,
The elves of luck inhabiting the breaking of morning fast,
The eyes and hands that probed the mind of God,
The body-mind of man,
Great were the probers for truth in the vanished day of our glory,
Before the coming of the melting fire,
Before the coming of our shame,
Before the time of deformity,
When we walked upright under
The skies of winged thunder power
Filled the roads with the gods of our cars,
Before the (second) great fall,
When the cash of our hands was fire,
Before the invasion of the other-market people,
Before worth dissolved in our hands
And the pentagonal anger of retribution arose,
The titan war of buttons,
Might in the heart of earth
Before the earthquake of dissolving fire
Mountain fought mountain,
We in the poverty of our deformities,
Who shall survive, remember the glory of our homes
While the money of our hands still rang true,
Who shall conquer now,
What good the power of retribution,
In this, the agony of our latter days,
Shall we all perish,

The invisible kills
And the invisible is everywhere,
Eternal,
The half-lives of our lives
Fractioned by the esoteric halving of eternity,
In the poverty of our diminishment
We sit by the waters of Huron and remember former glories,
In the conjunction of Castro-Chrysler-Ford,
Red star and spangled banner
We shall meet our doom . . . .

Grace Shinell

ATLANTIS DISCOVERED:
MEET THE SKYSCRAPER PEOPLE OF THE BURNING WEST

As told by the Reverend Sorrel Downs

HAVE YOU EVER overheard your friends describing you? Can you recall discussing somebody whom you knew only by popular report? In
fairness, any attempt to talk about the legendary Skyscraperans should
bring to mind these unlicensed confabulations.* Just as we may not recognize ourselves in our friend's descriptions, just as we may feel an acquaintance has made too much of an isolated instance, just so should
our judgments of the Skyscraperans be tempered by the realization that
we, in relation to them, are remote and estranged commentators. In assessing them we run the risk of being like strangers—intolerant and critical of differences, and like friends—competitive and defensive about
what we have in common. Certainly if the humans of the 4th millennium test our understanding so sorely, then the humans of the 1st and
2nd millennia must too.

If we want our knowledge to be respected, we should admit what we
do not know. Above all, we should be wary of assessing appearances. I
have attempted to distinguish between fact and theory and to give pre-
cedence to the former, for there are many details of Skyscraperan life
that can be ascertained through the fortunate discoveries of the last dec-
ade. Primarily it can be said that these savage people once thrived on the
bounteous shores of fabled Atlantis and that it was not through natural
disaster but rather through human agency that paradise was lost.

Ideally, historical analysis is premised on written material, but the
primitive Skyscraperans of Atlantis left no texts. Their use of writing appears to have been limited to odd jottings and titles. Nevertheless, I do
not think that it can serve any informative purpose to relegate—and
thereby reduce—the study of the Skyscraperans to what is rather dispar-
agingly designated as pre-history simply because theirs was a largely illiterate society. They left records and the Skyscraperan records are not as
easily misconstrued as tributes on monuments, carefully preserved (and
culled) administrative archives, or official biographies and other forms
of government propaganda. Unlike modern sophisticated societies, the
Skyscraperans were unconcerned about assuring themselves a favorable
place in history. Instead of monuments and archives, the Skyscraperans
left a profusion of waste matter, strewn along an unmistakable train of
devastation. Historians traditionally do not like to consider the litter of

---

*My recent experience with personal myth making has made me particularly sensi-
tive to the processes of exaggeration and invention. For example: although my colleagues did find me undernourished, I was not "deranged, unkempt, starved and
branded," as some uninformed individuals have insisted. Suffice it to say that the
state of my health during my mission among the primitive Atlanteans is best attest-
ed to by the work that I accomplished.

civilization, but such evidence is not easily distorted. Skyscraperan cities are still toxic, their farmlands still arid, their rivers still unpotable. For the scholar who is willing to literally dig into these remains—call her what you will—there are advantages in the way the Skyscraperans obviously lived—and died. The scale of their mistakes did not enable them to effect a cover up. Skyscraperan cities were not deserted by the people; rather, they fell into ruin as the people lived in them and, at last, metropolises and suburbs alike were left as open cemeteries. Evidence like this does not elude explanation, as some would maintain. It is self-explanatory. The Skyscraperans never had the wit or opportunity to write or rewrite their history. They met their end in an unpremeditated, sudden conflagration, and by its torchlight the past is still illumined for us.

For those who insist upon the greater validity of written records, there are several undoubtedly archaic and perhaps authoratative texts which we can examine. In the ruefully titled, *War to End All Wars*, we have what is widely considered to be a description of the final Skyscraperan debacle. Written many centuries after the war, its author, Lin Po, tells us that the people whom she identifies as the Skyscraperans preferred fire as a weapon. She says that the Skyscraperans in their desire to control the earth even fired at the moon, but because that body is made of ice, the fires were naturally quenched. Finally, she tells us that fires raged uncontrollably over the earth in all-consuming holocausts from which only a few sacral isles escaped.

The disputed *Diary of the Last Skyscraperan* adds to Lin Po's picture by informing us that housekeepers were incessantly beseeched to use bleaches, whiteners, softeners, and other solvents and purifiers to dissolve the soot and grime with which they were daily plagued and which the anonymous authoress specifically says fell from the sky. The writer of the *Diary* includes poignant references to the powerful goddess who the Skyscraperans believed had smote them, whom they called "Mother Nature."

It can be seen from the above that *The War to End All Wars* and the *Diary* corroborate each other to an extent that would seem to validate the content of each. In the same way the scarcely credited *Journal of a Voyager to the Ends of the Earth* adds its information. According to this source the Skyscraperan towers were constructed in an effort to cleanse the atmosphere, which the *Diary* tells us was the bane of housekeepers! The suggestion has been frequently made that the term "Skyscrapers," and thus the name of the people themselves, derives from this fanciful explanation. But what was once considered fanciful has become known fact. The horde of Rocksy Palace pictographs, which have recently come to light, prove that "Skyscraper" was the original name for the towers. The appelation was in common use throughout the second millennium, and even before the discovery of the engravings, it was preserved for us in the formerly discredited annals of the *Voyager*!

Although scarcely considered history, it is useful to reassess the reports of Climactic I, who claimed she had voyaged to the ends of the earth and discovered the reemergence of Atlantis from the sea. This charismatic adventuress unfortunately couched what could have been carefully detailed, routine reports in rather flamboyant and even romantic language. While we must strain to ignore Climactic's excesses, we are nevertheless indebted to her zeal, for who else but a pirate turned missionary could have given us so vivid a picture of Atlantis a scant 700 years after the great holocaust?

What Climactic found on the far side of the Atlantic was a continent so violently despoiled that she assumed it had been recently erupted. The extremely hot and gaseous air scorched the lungs of many of her followers and brought death to most within a few days. Water was scarce and foliage non-existent. Because of the limited food supplies, the only inhabitants were humans and other carnivores. While Climactic was unable to determine the age of the other carnivores, she noted that most of the humans were preadolescents who apparently survived just long enough in that pestilential land to bear offspring. Even Climactic gave up her mission and retired with a much reduced following to write up her experience.

Although the Skyscraperans were commonly illiterate, there were some poets among them, and we have a few of their verses, inscribed on a nearly indestructible clay, which was fortunately hard-baked in the holocaust. As might be expected, Skyscraperan poetry is on the level of doggerel but the sentiments are revealing. The poems are often idolatrous, revering in particular non-humans, including horses, birds, cats and dogs. It was not, therefore, out of hate that the Skyscraperans abused other animals but rather out of envy, which as these poems reveal can take the form of love or hate. Unfortunately, when all the shards are considered they are not sufficient to piece together a code of morals or a philosophy of life, such as one could expect to find in the remnants of a civilized society.

It is this very real dearth that has even more regrettably led to the promulgation of far too much theory with which this assessment of facts hopes to contend. Admittedly, among the many conjectural evaluations that have been constructed recently, there are two that seem to be particularly well supported.

The first is the papyri theory. The Rocksy Palace pictographs provide not one but many illustrations of papyri. The papyri is sometimes bound and sometimes in loose scrolls. There are often shelves of bound papyri and tables stacked with loose sheaves and it is humans who are depicted in the act of reading these papyri. Indeed, so extensive is this evidence that, if only these pictures survived, some easily satisfied scholar might be tempted to conclude that the Skyscraperans were widely literate! But there are also other depictions: masses of people walk through streets littered with papyri, which they do not bother to pick up. The only logical reason for such odd behavior would seem to be ignorance—in other words, illiteracy. From their multitudinousness, these people would appear to be in the majority. Other individuals, who are recognizable as mendicants or merchants, can be seen putting the papyri to practical use, e.g., stuffing their shoes with it, wrapping fish in it. Again, one can only assume that because the average Skyscraperan was unable to read, she could find no better use for the papyri that came into her hands.

Of course, this raises the question of why papyri was freely disseminated to illiterate masses to be scattered in the streets. The answer is also found in the Rocksy Palace pictographs. These engravings depict hysterical people burning piles of papyri, while others of similar inclination throw papyri out windows or tear it to shreds. From this evidence scholars have deduced that papyri was normally intended for the use of the ruling classes. When these educated individuals were displaced in the frequent revolutions and counterrevolutions (antidisestablishmentarianism), their papyri was resentfully destroyed or scornfully distributed to the poor and illiterate masses. It is hoped that readable papyri will turn up in the future, but given the frequent devaluation of it by the Skyscraperans themselves, that is highly unlikely.

So, despite the reasonableness of the papyri theory, we are left with the inescapable conclusion that most Skyscraperan communications were carried on orally and visually. Considering the thoughtlessness of human speech, it is perhaps as well that what was spoken among the Skyscraperans was not recorded, and fortunately the loss of verbal records is compensated for by the work of eidetic artists. The capacity to render extraordinarily lifelike and intricately detailed pictures is not unusual among primitives. Skyscraperan artists painstakingly etched exacting images on "see-thrus," such as the Rocksy Palace pictographs, and the reading of these detailed pictures may have been a skill in itself.

I am indebted to the studies of Mother Epona Schimmel who has proposed a theory of visual literacy that is worthy of close consideration. She has correctly noted that the Rocksy Palace pictographs show various levels of artistic achievement. For example, the works rendered in color are also more advanced in lighting, composition and subject. Mother Schimmel believes that Skyscraperan artists improved their ability to sketch and color images and that their audiences also became more adroit at quickly interpreting images. Eventually, the audiences became "visually literate" and images alone were sufficient to tell them a complicated story. Although I did not immediately realize it myself, Mother Schimmel points out in a private correspondence to me that the Rocksy Palace engravings, when considered in sequence, unfold stories more or less as the pictures unroll. These stories, or picture chronicles as she calls them, also show development in focus, composition and subject. Applying conventional literary standards, Mother Schimmel finds more advanced story development in works of color than exists in black and white picture chronicles. She particularly cites the use of foreshortening techniques. Schimmel cautions that what may seem to us to be confus-

ing shifts in time and place may actually be a result of the faster pace de-
manded by the superior visual literacy of Skyscraperan viewers.

Lamentably, we may note the same confusing trend in modern writing
and a similar impatience in modern readers! Therefore, without more explanation, I offer this account of the Skyscraper People of the Burning
West, arrived at after extensive review of the Rocksy Palace engravings
and other pictorial evidence, taking into consideration Mother Epona
Schimmel's theories and making particular use of her dating system
based upon artistic development.

WARFARE

Among the Skyscraperans, warfare was a way of life for the average
man. From the pictures we can see that women in the main abstained.
The reasons for this will become obvious but it should be commented
upon now that the longer maturation period of males may not have
been recognized in Skyscraperan times. Eighteen-year-old striplings were
drafted into the armed services. At that tender age they were denied the
rowdy play periods that are so necessary to the developing boy. The result was a lifelong frustration that most often found expression in deadly serious warfare.

Not only were the youths of the society unnaturally stunted, so was
every other social potentiality because of the incessant warring. Even
weaponry (as well as more useful tools and amenities) remained relatively primitive. Basically the Skyscraperan insisted upon using the same
weapons as his stone age fathers: fire and rocks. The chief innovation
was the manufacture of missiles in regulated sizes, which could be more
conveniently transported and stored than natural rocks. Shaped for max-
imum air speed, these man-made missiles were often filled with combust-
ibles and launched from contraptions that were in effect giant-sized
mechanized slingshots.

From a translation of a subtitled pictograph, we learn that "Chemical
warfare was tried but the tactic backfired." The picture is unrecogniz-
able but it may show some form of new or maimed life. "Backfired"
may be a reference to a calculation of wind factors that may have turned the fire from the combustible chemicals in the wrong direction. One
thing is certain: the Skyscraperans could not have understood the ele-
mental magical properties of chemical potions or they never would have
unstopped them.

Psychological warfare also appears to have been in a dangerous rather
than an innocent infancy. There are depictions of spell casting but they
make clear that little was understood about sympathetic reaction or ex-
orcism. For example, in one depiction a robed figure stands behind an
altar. His face is contorted with rage and he points accusingly at the
heavens.

Notions of chivalry, if they existed, are hard to comprehend. Hiding
behind shields was apparently frowned upon in late Skyscraperan times,

but crouching inside of homes where the inhabitants were women and children was not. Indeed, sometimes the women and children were used as shields. There were no lines of battle, so there may have been no rules of warfare either. Surely no truce or peace could have lasted very long if a Skyscraperan credo (with accompanying pictures of numbered, uniformed combatants) expresses the thinking of the time. It reads: "The best defense is a good offense."

SOCIAL STRUCTURE

We may well ask then, what, if any, was the prevailing form of social order? We may gauge that in the chaos of revolution and counterrevolution the role of men was increasingly limited to that of defender, while the Skyscraperan woman attended to the more necessary and normal tasks of survival, such as food gathering and shelter construction. Modern sociologists will smile in recognition, for we have here a classic genesis with only one possible outcome—the emergence of gynocracy. Unfortunately, Skyscraperan society seems to have never progressed beyond a pre-gynocratic matriarchy.

A sure sign of matriarchy is the celebration of everyone's birth days on as frequent a basis as possible—that is, annually—and to the Skyscraperan matriarchy, a birth day was as worthy of commemoration as an historic victory. Schools and businesses were closed. Workers were excused from labor and, like the children, granted special favors and permitted to cavort in the streets.

EDUCATION

While some attempt at instruction was made, we are informed that the schools existed primarily to keep the children off the streets, which were unsafe. There were scheduled play periods, meal periods and frequent outings. An emphasis on the light hearted seems to have been stressed, particularly in the late Skyscraperan period when the social order was nearing collapse. What we would call games—not lessons—were taught. A significant translation informs us that students had to be urged to stay in school.

MATRIARCHAL RELIGION

There appears to have been an almost militant movement in support of progeneration. Calling themselves "Pro-Lifers," women and children marched in the streets with pictures of fetuses. Under these circumstances great reverence was paid to the moon diety Sin, who as we know regulates the menstrual cycle. There are frequent references to "Houses of Sin," the "Attraction of Sin," "Sin City," "Sin-loving," and "hordes of Sinners." The sun was also accorded its earthly representative. Because the Skyscraperans believed in the "Glorification of the Common Man," Skyscraperan matriarchs firmly pursued a policy of electing Sun Kings. The term of these Sun Kings, like all Sun Kings, depended entirely

upon their popularity. Modern women can well sympathize with their
Skyscraperan sisters over the evident problem of finding suitable candi-
dates. None of the reigns of the Skyscraperan Sun Kings lasted more
than a dozen years. This was so despite the fact that Kings were secluded
in a place called the White House, where it was hoped that the color
might reflect upon its inhabitants. Although the Sun Kings were supposed to be elected by women's suffrage—a right for which the women
fought—the names of a few kings reveal the possibility of patrilinear as-
cendancy, e.g., there are several John's sons and Jack's sons, which may
only go to prove the old adage, "Like father, like son."

AMAZON SEPARATISTS

Other sects besides Sinners left their mark on Skyscraperan society,
and none must have been more opposed to the tradition of exalted con-
sorts than the Amazons. If one is to judge by references to Amazons in
the picture chronicles, the sect appears to have been a growing one, particularly in the latter part of the Skyscraperan epoch. The addition of an
ever greater number of symbolic Amazon stars to the Skyscraperan flag
(with no change in the number of stripes) may reflect this increase in
Amazons and, in that case, they would clearly have been a majority party. If we accept this proposition, it is difficult to explain the prevalence
of practices that would have been offensive to the Amazon majority.

The dilemma remains unresolved and has caused some scholars to
doubt there ever were Amazons living in second millennium Atlantis,
even as a minority. They point out that modern Amazons would rather
perish than consort. But this sort of scholarly carping has been thoroughly squelched by recent findings. The new, unassailable evidence proves
that Amazon puberty rites were routinely performed in the latter part
of the second millennium. A sequence of see-thru pictographs has been
found showing a young woman with her right breast removed. She
proudly bares her star scar and smiles encouragingly to a long line of
women, dressed in loose, white linen gowns, who await their turns.
Significantly, the pictures are entitled, "It Could Happen to YOU." In a
further sequence, the young woman is seen exercising her right arm and
in particular, demonstrating the freedom of reach that she now has as a
result of the operation. We are left with the impression that she has
come through as a spirited Amazon should, and that in a few days she
will again take up her bow with an unimpeded aim.

A FEMALE PANTHEON

Whether government was in its matriarchal or pre-gynocratic stage, religion played an important part in the governance of the populace. From
the many depictions of "The Marion One," it would appear that nursing
mothers were religiously worshipped, at least in early times. By late Skyscraperan III, there appears to have been a veritable gynocratic hagiocra-
cy in the offing. By the end of the second millennium, the ruling panthe-

on included such diverse d   ties as: CIA, Goddess of Wisdom; AMA, Goddess of Health; GE, Goddess of the Home; USA, Goddess of Earth; NASA, Goddess of the Sky, and ASE and NYSE, who were the Twin Goddesses of Prosperity. We find from the translations that CIA and USA, as well as sometimes AMA and NASA, sent their assistance to war-torn areas. This statement is further corroborated by several depictions of priestesses, symbolically dressed in white, who are shown bathing the wounds of warriors.

DEATH AND MORALITY

One might think that cannibals would observe few death rites, but among the Skyscraperans the period of mourning was prolonged and elaborated. In particular, reliquaries were popularly cherished. Although some organs were kept alive by transplanting them in living recipients, others were idealized in art forms such as crude sculpture and pottery. This latter practice probably had a subsidiary cultural benefit in that it led to the development of the visual arts. In the late Skyscraperan period, picture chronicles were commissioned to depict the deceased in all their lifetime activities. The pictures were displayed in special boxes kept in the main room of each dwelling.

Of an evening, the survivors gathered around the box, and by means of turning dials, wound the roll of pictures past a viewing screen that made up one side of the box. The boxes were often works of art in themselves, decoratively carved, and polished to a shiny finish. They were called "televisions," and from this one may suppose there was an effort to induce telepathic communications with the dead, as well as spectral visions through communal concentration on the lifelike pictures. Whereas rich families employed the talents of famous artists and paid for the additional cost of color pictures, poor families could afford only inferior black and white renderings of their beloved ones.

Because of the difficulties in conceiving of a people who devoured their own dead and then sat around revering their memory in maudlin detail, incautious commentators have attributed modern sensibilities to the savages who dwelt on the ravaged shores of Atlantis so long ago. It has been suggested that their unsavory foodstuffs, which included their own kindred, were donated by the grieving families to be redistributed for anonymous consumption. This is an interesting and, under the circumstances, even attractive idea, but unfortunately I can find no evidence for a marketing procedure that concealed the identity of corpses. Of course, Skyscraperans never accorded non-humans, such as cattle, fowl and fish, identity. These animals were bred to be eaten (hippi were bred to be ridden but were also eaten) and the records of the brief existence of these species are as blunt as was the means of their execution. They are simply described by size and weight and their carcasses are literally numbered among countless millions whom the Skyscraperans consumed. Considering these facts, it is perhaps to the credit of the Skyscraperans that they did not merely enumerate their own kind and kindred while they fed upon them. For civilized seed eaters such as ourselves, it is difficult to understand the more superficial aspects of a violent, fearful society, but in regard to the Skyscraperans, I think that we may succeed in comprehending their display of necrophilism. Theirs was an overt expression of guilt, which eventually took artistic form—so socially acceptable was their carrion diet!

THE SKYSCRAPER BUILDINGS

Home to a Skyscraperan was a besieged fortress—at least home for a lucky Skyscraperan. Pictures show masses of hapless refugees, and the captions succinctly describe them as "victims of war." The towers that sheltered the lucky ones were divided into dozens of small units, the windows of which were protectively sealed. Narrow stairways provided the only access and egress but few inhabitants could have cared to venture outside. Of those who did, still fewer would have survived to return. In all respects, the towers were built and maintained for habitation during long periods of siege. Each was constructed with one or more storage wells. The depth of the wells was from basement to roof and each well was equipped with a cart that could be raised or lowered on a pulley. Although we cannot be sure what was stored in the wells, they are remarkably similar to the silos of modern granaries. Wisely, the silos were located inside the buildings, while on the roofs were tanks for the accumulation of rain water. The towers were undoubtedly self-sufficient and perhaps efficient housing. Waste matter was probably tossed into the war-related conflagrations that raged nearby. Certainly heating posed no problem, and since fire was always available, fire places for cooking went out of use. Decorative or votive non-working models were sometimes retained or sentimentally installed at winter solstice time.

CURRENCY

The repeated cycles of peace and war created a spiral of plenty and want that in turn created a vortex of unending greed. It is interesting to see how greed will always trick itself. Picture chronicles of Skyscraperans show that in addition to barter shells worn on their bodies and clothes, Skyscraperans accumulated wads of paper. This paper was apparently of great value and could be exchanged for almost anything. Modern students of economics will shudder at the thought of the inevitable, which will have immediately occurred to them, whereas the uninitiated reader may sensibly inquire, "But what if there was a great fire that consumed all the paper—who would know who was rich or poor?" Certainly, among Skyscraperans, there must have been many disruptions affecting property ownership, but it is more astonishing to consider the potentiality of fraud. We can only suppose that if it was possible to convince people that a scrap of paper was equal to a well-stocked larder or adequate shelter, then it was also possible to arbitrarily inflate or deflate the expressed value of the paper, which in itself had no intrinsic value. We know that the people of one territory would not accept the paper of the people from another territory, and from this we may conclude that each had cause to doubt the other's worth.

Nevertheless, many a Skyscraperan walked around thinking herself rich because she possessed a paper book that recorded the amount of paper she owned, which was too voluminous to carry with her. Or perhaps, in a final irony, she had contrived to exchange some of her paper for stock in a trading emporium. This arrangement did not mean that she would actually get any of the trading emporium's stock. All she would receive was another piece of paper, which was itself obtained at a charge from intermediaries who were appropriately called "Brokers." This same woman would still go on believing herself rich, although she might not possess an abode or a bushel of grain that she could call her own. Instead she would be forced to continue exchanging a certain amount of her paper for a place to sleep and daily food. The cooking of this food, which was generally done at ground level, would cost her another sum in establishments especially created for the cooking and serving of food. Service cost extra. The generic name given these places is at least indicative of some respite and refuge from the aimlessness and homelessness of the average Skyscraperan's condition. "Restaurants" were storerooms to which a hungry, homeless person might retire for repast, although sadly we must suspect that this name, too, may have been misleading and intended mainly for sales appeal. The surviving depictions of "restaurants," "rest rooms," and the like do not appear to be the kind of places that we would call home.

HEALTH CONDITIONS

There is good evidence that many a plague was visited upon the Skyscraperans. There were public warnings not to drink the water or to breathe the air. As their name implies, the Skyscraperans had an original (but also futile) solution for the latter problem. Their famous towers were apparently constructed in naive and desperate efforts to reach what they supposed was the roof of the earth. In this they were spurred on by their scientists who urged them to leave the earth for a totally ambiguous place called "outer space."

Even after the Skyscraperans discovered that they could never reach the roof of the sky, they continued adding story on top of story in increasingly towering, shaky edifices, simply to get away from the litter and stench of their streets. These thoroughfares were, like their waterways, open sewers, owing to the indiscriminate habits of the people and their domesticated animals who were not often distinguishable from each other, the latter shamefully acquiring the habits of the former.

But of all the plagues visited upon the Skyscraperans, the worst was very likely an infestation of enormous bugs, which appeared at any season and in any terrain. The specie is happily unknown to us but depictions show that it was capable of devouring the countryside, cutting down trees and even eating through hillsides, leaving only a barren trail to mark what may be questionably called its progress. The insects also left a wake of noxious fumes; at least that is the impression one gains from a close study of several engravings. The fumes may have been a defense mechanism, but that is not to say that these bugs were retiring when challenged. To judge by the pictorial evidence, they were among the most aggressive bugs ever to crawl the earth. And, most remarkably, they did so in armor, bearing gleaming weapons, and wearing regimental emblems and other medallions. There are battle scenes showing squadrons of bugs on the march. Their sheer aggressiveness often caused them to meet in head-on confrontations that left one or more combatants lifeless. Sometimes the loss of life was so great that mutilated carcasses were simply stacked or left strewn over the countryside. These pictures have not been shown to the public as the sight of so much dried blood is difficult to view.*

Humans, with their carrion instincts, were the chief scavengers of these rotting carcasses. They can be seen, sometimes with their children, picking over the hulking wrecks. It is with obvious delight that humans viewed the bug wars and they frequently appear as bystanders rather than as contenders. Their attitude is at least understandable as they were themselves the favorite prey of these enormous insects. Women, men, children, and even dogs can be seen through the bubble heads and glassy eyes of these voracious bugs, as they are being swallowed whole and alive. Some of the bugs were capable of digesting as many as 50 humans at a single time.

The specie varied greatly in form, color and size. To an entomologist, this multivariousness offers fascinating possibilities for conjecture. In classifying the bug, some experts have termed it"the mastodon of insects." Philologists have come up with a still more startling consideration. From a careful study of picture captions, they believe the Skyscraperan word for these insects was "cars." I am compelled to add that this word appears in a reference that can be translated as follows: "Early in the 20th century *cars* killed off horses." Indeed, our small-brained, apteryx ancestors do seem to have disappeared from 20th century scenes, whereas engravings of their brutal enslavement are quite common in the preceeding century.

CLIMATE AND AGRICULTURE

The uniformly torrid continent, known in antiquity as Atlantis, once had a variable climate to which the continent's geographical features contributed. In the early second millennium, there were snow-capped moun-

---

* Although it is not a dispute I care to enter, some observers have erroneously maintained that much of the blood is merely rusting armor. I cannot see that this explanation in any way mitigates the effect on the sensitive viewer. Moreover, Skyscraperan metallurgy was sufficiently advanced to retard oxidation for quite a long period of time.

tains, icy rivers, fertile plains, dense forests and teeming swamplands. As these geographical features were gradually depleted or demolished by incessant warfare, the Atlantean climate grew hotter and drier. War-related fires contributed to the intense heat and left a seared terrain of ashes and dust. Recognizing the problem, the Skyscraperans desperately established fire fighting brigades in every settlement, but these often-volunteer units were neither sufficiently trained nor equipped to control the combustible elements in the weaponry of the time. By the end of the second millennium, once-provident Atlantis was shrouded in smoke so thick that some locales received less than 75% of normal sunlight. The inhabitants were forced to farm indoors and the windows of every skyscraper were crowded with stunted growths planted in pots of every description. But a people as resourceful as the Skyscraperans were in no danger of starving. As we already know, they resorted to cannibalism.

COSMETICS AND DRESS

With the reader's forebearance, I must now embark upon a most distasteful subject in unvarnished detail. The lack of adequate hair, feathers or scales, as well as the uniformly dull coloring of the human body, was compensated for among the Skyscraperans by the most sordid means imaginable—even for the human mind. Rejected as a viable species, homo sapiens during the Skyscraperan era avenged themselves on others. Denied by nature, they adorned themselves as they would have liked to look. They dressed in the skins of snakes and lizards, in the hides of cows and horses, in the furs of seals and cats, in the feathers of ostriches and peacocks. Weakened through evolution, they made jewelry of others' horns, teeth, and claws. Environmentally endangered, they oiled their own exposed skins with the jellies and fats of every other living creature from bees to whales. The scent of their own glands so displeased them that they perfumed their malodorous bodies with the musk of deer and the scent of wild flowers. Body painting was perhaps a more innocent means of covering their unnatural nakedness; unfortunately it was not sufficiently resorted to.

GAMES, SPORTS AND CELEBRATIONS

The long boring sieges led to the invention of at least one parlor game which, from the prevalence of its fixtures, must have achieved great popularity. Each parlor, and sometimes other rooms, had one of the game sets. "Telephone" sets included a dial with holes for each of the human's ten fingers. The holes were numbered one through zero and 24 of the 48 letters of the Skyscraperan alphabet were also indicated. Like the ubiquitous "television," the "telephone" may have been used for telepathic communications. Some experimenters have determined that the game can be used for a simple form of I Ching or astrological forecasting.

Number games do appear to have been extremely popular among the largely illiterate Skyscraperans, and one game was played so frequently that it was carried around by means of a strap fastened to the wrist. Larger versions, perhaps for more players, were kept in every home and conveniently arranged on tables or hung on walls.

Not surprisingly, Skyscraperan sports were reminiscent of warfare. Objects were hurled either at a target or at the opposing side. Hand-to-hand grappling, kicking and wrestling were also permissible. Again, from such activities women in the main abstained. They appear to have preferred rhythmic, individual exercises with dance-like but often arduous motions rather than the group competitions of the men and boys.

Because of the fuming fires outdoors, and generally pestilential atmosphere, sports and celebrations were frequently conducted indoors. Even so, sports spectators managed to cheer, carouse and fight. Curiously, and especially by today's standards, social gatherings were subdued affairs. People simply crowded into small dark rooms, where most had to remain standing. As the always smoke-filled air became increasingly noxious, disposable inhalators were brought out and passed around to each party-goer. These were small white tubes through which air was sucked and, according to the advertisements, filtered. Sometimes the tubes themselves were deliberately ignited as a sardonic prank.

At such times the human party-goers dressed up in their best finery. Perhaps it shows an unexpected consideration that they invited only an occasional cat or dog, for it was in the luxurious furs and ruffled feathers of every other species that humans prided and preened themselves on these occasions. The abhorrent extremes of human envy have been sufficiently detailed, but the extremes of their absurd emulation have not been mentioned. In addition to wearing the actual skins of other animals, Skyscraperans sometimes donned offensively representational costumes. Unable to effectively mimic the speech and manners of their betters, these humans clowned, grimaced and babbled, all the while imagining themselves to be convincing or at least amusing.

From all of the foregoing, I trust that the reader has gained a clear impression of Skyscraperan life, death and faith. In the process she may also have acquired an awesome respect for her own race's struggling emergence and triumphal survival against incredible odds. Yet, as would-be masters of the hippi, it would seem that the Skyscraperans, even more than other humans, defeated themselves. The same evidence leads us to a further conclusion that may seem surprising in view of the ignorance, disorder and unproductive conflict among the Skyscraperans: We must conclude that the Skyscraperans' most damning vice was over-achieving. They were such selfish producers that in the final analysis they were over-achievers of self-destruction.

*

Sorrel Downs is a frequent contributor to the Mission Society's Bulletin. *She is presently at work on a book-length analysis of the Human Problem, entitled "The Grasping Thumb."*

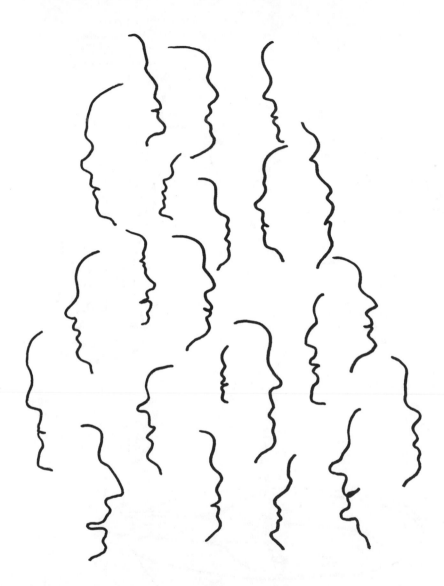

Figure 1

The natural diversity of human countenances coupled with the unnatural ability to drastically alter facial expression tends to confuse and even overwhelm members of other species. In confrontation, humans quickly employ dissimulating tactics to obtain an unfair advantage.

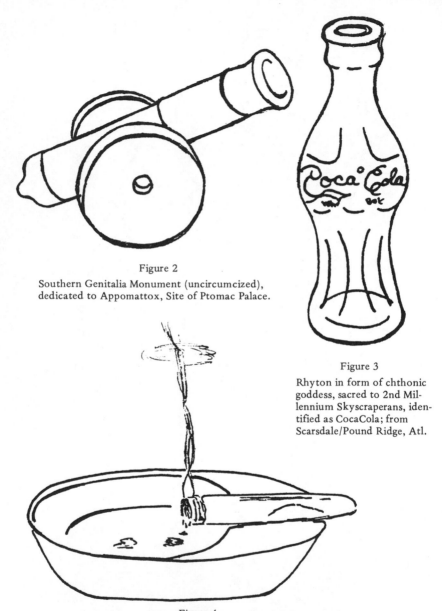

Figure 2

Southern Genitalia Monument (uncircumcized),
dedicated to Appomattox, Site of Ptomac Palace.

Figure 3

Rhyton in form of chthonic
goddess, sacred to 2nd Millennium Skyscraperans, identified as CocaCola; from
Scarsdale/Pound Ridge, Atl.

Figure 4

An artist's rendering of the "ash dish" in use. Primitive Atlanteans
still "smoke" tobacco leaves, but the custom, which is dangerous to
life and property, has been banned in civilized districts of Atlantis.

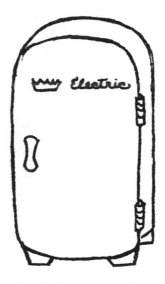

Figure 5
Vertical sarcophagus with family
crest. Note handle and hinges for
ease of opening. Rock City, Atl.

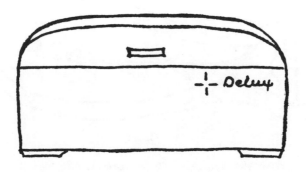

Figure 6
Horizontal sarcophagus; also has hinges (un-
seen) and convenient handle. Rock City, Atl.

Figures 7, 8, 9, 10, 11

Reliquary Dishes. The Skyscraperan diet was varied to the point of being indiscriminate. Even small boney creatures, bearing scales or feathers, were considered suitable fare for a Skyscraperan banquet. The dead body, whole or butchered, was
served in clay molds like these, which were once thought to facilitate cooking. Organs, including hearts, livers, brains, and tongues, were considered "delicacies." The
reliquary in the form of a human hand is somewhat unusual.

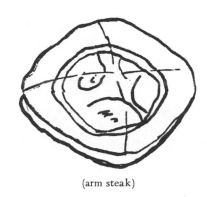

(arm steak)

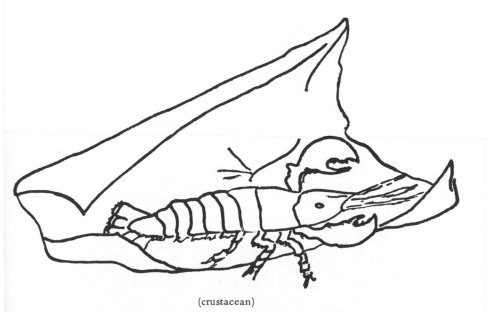

(crustacean)

Figures 12, 13

Mummy shrouds like these wrappings must have proved ineffective in preserving the dead. Pyramid power appears to have been unknown in the 2nd Millennium.

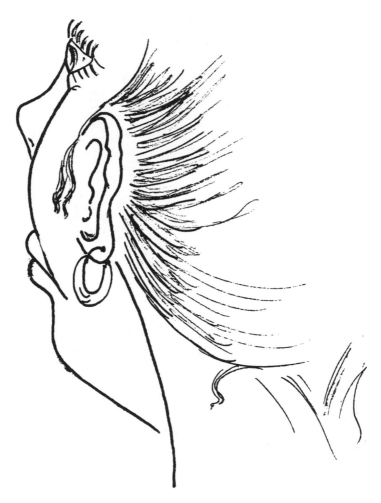

Figure 14
Beardless, female homosapien with gold ring
secured through her ear lobe to prevent theft.

Figure 15

Two Skyscraperan housekeepers exhibiting marked differences in attitude. The one on the left is described as "grumpy." He has apparently just returned from an unsatisfactory shopping trip; note that he is still wearing a nightcap and bedroom slippers. The housekeeper on the right probably still has his hair in curlers underneath his nightcap, but he has at least put on a dress and shoes and is about to begin the day's work with zeal. Described as "happy," he is probably on drugs, which was the approved treatment for manic-depressive tendencies, commonly found among 20th century houseworkers.

Diane Glancy
LEGEND

Indians who wander
from the tribe
become bears.

I must ask your permission, bear,
to kill you.
You are brother.

You come too close at night.
I hear your breath,
know the wetness of your mouth.

I need you, bear.
Your fur and meat,
your claws as ornaments
for my neck.

I must have your warmth
but cannot wander
and become bear.

My arrow ready,
I ask your permission.

Tom Hansen

COMPLAINT
(found poem)

Emil Victor, in the County of Brown
and State of South Dakota,
on the 3rd day of July, A.D. 1909,
with force and arms, then and there
did commit the crime of Murder,
committed as follows: That at said time and place
said Emil Victor, the defendant, did wilfully,
unlawfully and feloniously and of his deliberate
and premeditated design and malice aforethot to
effect the death of one Mildred Christie,
a female human being,
did make an assault upon the said Mildred Christie
with a certain gun, commonly called a revolver,
loaded with gun powder and leaden balls,
then and there held in his hands,
he, the said Emil Victor, did then and there
unlawfully, wilfully and feloniously,
and of his deliberate and premeditated design to
effect the death of her, the said Mildred Christie,
make an assault upon her, said Mildred Christie,
and did discharge and shoot off said revolver,
loaded as aforesaid, at and upon the head of her,
the said Mildred Christie,
thereby crushing and breaking into the skull
and brain of her, the said Mildred Christie,
and inflicting upon and in the head of her,
the said Mildred Christie,
certain mortal wounds,
of and from which said mortal wounds,
the said Mildred Christie did
on the 3rd day of July, 1909,
linger and die.

135

Brown Miller
ITS HOUR COME ROUND AT LAST

From ground that once
grew Hiroshima grow
plants manufacturing
Mazdas, Dodge Colts,

restaurants welcoming
Diner's Club, Mastercharge,
chains of Mr. Doughnut
revolving day and night.
Little was rebuilt.

It all had to be new
to cover the smudge.
In these clean buildings
time-released capsules
are swallowed reverently.

The new money serves
as scar tissue so no one
recalls the numb splendor.

Hiroshima hides in its
business address, summons
executives who court
clients with dinners and
gambling and massage.

Survivors do not survive.
August 6, 1945: the dawn
came as a bomb, born
inconveniently. There
was no room at the inn.

Layle Silbert / photo

Morty Sklar
POEM TO THE SUN

You want to sit here and write a poem,
here in Rossi's Cafe on Gilbert,
main drag trucks early a.m.
across from end of March puddle empty lots
across from sun

       hop skip and jump from
rooftop shingle to puddle to semi windshield
shatter, in the dust diffused in window,
home fries eggs sunnyside grease air in Rossi's,
ninety-three million miles

       beamed down, twenty-five feet from a
puddle, ye gads, ninety-three
million miles to a puddle, no, not yet
O Great Starship, don't beam me
back

       . . . the snow
has just melted here,
light spreading like a cosmic *good* virus,
glinting off auburn coffee, splashed on
the floor tossed around in mop
with radio wave mix from shelf
transistor

       . . . You want to be
a living crystal receiver, here,
goddamn,
       40 billion trillion miles from nowhere,

next to a puddle,
next to the sun.

James Grabill
THE NIGHT ENERGY MOVES IN WAVES

I

The solid night is also energy.
Potential hovers. Blue suns grow
in the night sky of each cell.

II

What are we giving up, that we can't
do without? The radio brings a dust
from Europe. Its ocean moves in waves,
carried by slower waves, and slower waves,
until they are solid. Its luminous fish
are like blue flames from another century.
Breathing, we give off a light
of salt and rainwater.

III

What are the two lives we live?
Action and consideration, the ground
and air, the dragonfly eats
and turns, in a further life
of astral beauty.

IV

I have been waiting for things
to change, but they grow.
Each step deepens, then resides.
In the house, books swim back
under the vegetation. A koan
talks from the clocks of Monday.
In the storm, the seven bodies
bend in the grove of trees.

cont'd

V

A frequency moves like wheat.
Steel glows in the yards.
Who has been telling us to do things?
Who can we love by sitting here, standing,
talking together? The music we love
passes through us like the whales.
For a few hours, our cells
move in that ocean.

Rolf Jacobsen
BRIEFING

God said: The small ones.
Let them come unto me.
Psst! All small ones. Over here. Line up
small hands silk socks thoughts
light and air small words and deeds
small houses small countries small animals and flowers
foxglove and honeysuckle. We'll let
the big ones make their own way. All small ones
feel welcome. Not so afraid, then.
Come on.
Come on. And take the canary with you,
because now we have to think a bit
about what's happening. We must
be stronger on the earth steadier
on our feet or they'll take us
and put us in the sack
all together—one after the other
each silk sock each shadow light and air
everything that makes the earth green
and the sky blue
small houses small countries small messages
and small letters bees
and ants and earthworms
do not be blown away but stay
where you are.
Watch out
for your heads.
Don't lose your grip. Remember
that the earth spins
round and round
and round and round
and that everything that is
comes again
—me too. Said God.

transl. from the Norwegian by Roger Greenwald

David Hilton
1952

In 7th grade the teacher blasted
her whistle and we dove
under our desks. Our hands
made frail bony helmets
to cut the risk of brain damage.
We raised our asses against a wall
of windows. The sun was warm,
we closed our eyes. The incandescent
glass-filled hurricane
would only stab our butts funny
like when Porky sits on a spike
and zooms in crazy pain
right up through a cloud.

Our foreskulls
drilled the floor
in blind, burrowing *asanas*—
most important to keep
absolutely quiet. *Not a whisper!*
the teacher would whisper
because the monster might hear us
and know straight where to come.

Our little assholes fibrillated
as if caught up on a stick.
The teacher must have studied
that trembling—but she never
explained to us boys
how our quickening balls
hung down like soft cocoons
before the Atom Bomb!

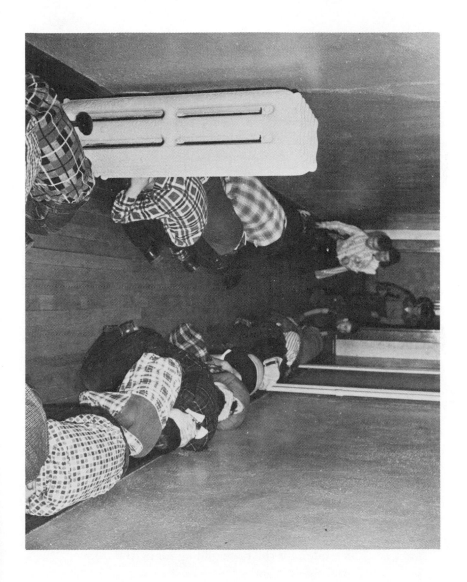

Anonymous / photo / provided by the Iowa Historical Society

Cleveland Latham

MY STUDENTS IN MILITARY SCHOOL

My words crawl free
of the space behind the podium,
bringing with them
to the center of the room
the dissonant treble of their voice.
I sit among the boys,
my legs stretching before me
to adopt their postures. Their
desks gather about in a village of darkened
shacks, having sprung up where they will.
But the boys themselves hold back,
their bald eyes only tumuli,
their defensive arms taut
and stretched by hard veins.

When I gave them my poem of home,
my family clustered when my mother died,
I asked them to see where I'd come from,
from beyond these hills that have risen around me
like bunkers, from beyond my dormitory apartment
that quakes hourly with their bells
and their parades, their days marked
by a schedule that allows no moment
for the cadence of the dying.
They winced at the biting intimacy
resting on the paper before them.

Each evening, I burrow into that apartment
dragging behind a dormitory, its halls
clouded by the light gliding along the floor
through cracks under their doors,
light that pulls with it the chilling vapor
of our mysterious plight. In my rooms
or in theirs, I fidget—and the boys
veer around me as if I were a traffic light

stalled on yellow. They head for each other
or for the phone, their sentences and algebra
etched in a hand they cannot recognize
when they return.

Weary in my office, I tally my students'
hours with me in cords of letters and numbers.
For my grade book, their names are their
fathers', their first names only an initial—
stuttering, angry Martin becomes only an M
period.
His papers furl around the night I stole
upon him in his room, crying with
some private anger; he writes
madly, he told me, trying to get at
"what you want."
I want that rasping night, Martin; I can hold it
as close to me as I hold my own windbreaker. I want
your letters home; I can hear with you
the frail ringings of your messages of love,
going on and on, unanswered, through the wires
and cables we have invented to deny our distances.

One paper lies on my desk unclaimed,
a deadline somehow unmanaged,
this boy travelling today for home.
He had left his gray dress coat
in my apartment,
draped over a kitchen chair like my wife's apron
when she has tidied away her day.
The coat's smooth breast, bare of medals,
shines anyway under the yellow light;
the sleeves have been raked clean of their rank.
Why should a boy leave love behind
when a home's love has died,

his mother and father calling him
to his own charred skeleton and their bones?

My wife greets me with empty arms,
her face pulled tight with smiling.
At night, on the sofa, we cuddle into ourselves,
knees raised against our chins,
our arms bound around our legs in a circle
holding together our two bodies.

For my class, the boys have memorized
a clipped response, and as they pare my days
into concise notes, crowding as much as they can
into the outside margin, their hands lunge steadily
away from their hearts while I grope around
among the lives of other people's sons
who cannot be mine.

Floyd Skloot
RULES OF THE GAME

1. Everyone will begin in the same dark place.

2. Light, which is The Finish, will be visible through tiny openings at the farthest reaches of long tunnels.

3. You may start moving only when a pea-green gauze is slipped over those openings, filtering the light.

4. Options will abound as you proceed through tunnels:
   a) North, South, East, or West
   b) Up or Down
   c) Up and North
   d) Up and East
   e) Down and West
   f) Etc.

5. Do not touch walls.

6. Do not go backwards (a tunnel passed through will be a tunnel closed).

7. There will be one (1) carafe of sweetwater at the halfway point in every right tunnel.

8. Keep moving (being still too long will cause your eyes to cloud over in here).

9. Do not talk to anyone you meet. *

10. A pistol, lantern without battery, and boots are mandatory and will be issued to you at the beginning of the game. In addition, you will be allowed two (2) optional pieces of equipment, selected from among the following:
   a) two (2) bullets
   b) lantern battery
   c) First-Aid Kit

     d) empty canteen

     e) three (3) matches

Please note that one (1) exchange of optional equipment will be permitted during the game.

11. A period of time not to exceed thirty (30) seconds may be designated by you as time when none of the above rules shall apply.

12. There are no procedures for quitting.

*The penalty for violating Rule 9 is, you must proceed together with whomever you talk to, from that point. Remembering Rules 6 and 8, you can see that your options become limited when you involve yourself with another player. The penalty for violating any other rule is elimination from the game.

Byron Burford / "Women Making Bullets" / encaustic on canvas

Jimmy Santiago Baca
A BEAUTIFUL DAY

I wonder if we are at the edge of existence?
If this society's inner force
has broken down like a cart's wheel
and if the dream that pulls us forth like a horse
has been set free
and returned to the hills
where other people with more honorable spirits than ours
can lure it to their outstretched hands
and it will carry them through the desert
to a place where there is water and trees?

What obscure love gave us wealth
we have beaten like a dog with a whip.
We have starved it,
made carpets of its fur
and jewels of its bones. Its skull gapes at us
down the silence of each street at dawn,
and the clash of traffic at noon
sounds its dying shriek.

One could follow the horrors of the past fifty years
as if counting beads on a rosary
and counting dollar bills. What gods have we evoked
but bombs and banks?

I saw something similar to a nuclear bomb go off.
One morning a person has a dove in a small cage.
The sun wrestles in trees
like a child on papa's bed on sunday
when neither has to work or go to school.
It is a beautiful day.
The grass is as luxurious
as a beautiful young woman in a green dress.
This person goes into the house and shortly returns
with a double barrel shot gun. Opens the cage gate.
Jams the barrel against the dove.

Shoves it to a corner. The dove cannot move.
Both black barrels completely cover the dove.
A few feathers fray out of the rim.
Squeeze the trigger.

                        There is no bird,
                        only the smell of smoke.

We are the bird.

Helen Redman / oil painting

William Oandasan
UKOM & NO'M

1

the blackberry grows sweet
plump and juicy near William's Creek
where it bloomed aeons ago
when we tasted its flavor first

2

an emptied bottle of Coors
ditched in moonlight at Inspiration Point
shines with the numbing skin
of drunkards freezing in snow

3

home sleeps 1,000 miles northwest
when i palm the green jade
from the stream east of Aunt Mary's
smells of redwood surface again

4

near the foot of slopes fen-
cing the valley on the north
the reservation rests quietly
as resistance burned out

5

through the heart of Covelo
Commercial Boulevard parades past
a gas station, cafe, saloon, store, etc.
signs of the empire

cont'd

6

across the street nearly mute
an old woman moans alone
inside the Buckhorn saloon
cowboys drink up and stomp

7

in color and strength
three Philippino gaming cocks
appear from across the water
in the yard pullets cluck excitedly

8

between the round piece of green jade
and my firm touch
Medicine Hill so far away
resembles a horizonline at dawn

9

north by south, west from east
an invisible but historical line
cuts across the valley's lives
sharp like bloodlines

10

across the salty distance
and decades of grief since Hiroshima
clouds of holocaust fall
over the valley and earth

11
next to the road into Covelo
Mr. A.'s spread lays for desire,
greed, deceit, shame, alcohol, distrust
all's now forgotten though not forgiven

12
Turner Creek's the core of winter
except when blackberry buds flare again
and transform the light of spring
fire enough for another year

Sally Fisher
ASH WEDNESDAY AGAIN

The believers in God believe him to be slow.
This is the hard time of the year, and God is slowest.

On Broadway blackened snow clings like moss to the curbs.
Signs of spring are rhubarb, asparagus, expensive strawberries.
At the newsstand, through the halftone dots in a pound of
                                        newsprint
another earth-turn, and the day's harvest of numbers
interpreting accident, vice, human decision.

          This is an Algonquin story I tell to
          my children: Once there was a year when
          spring did not come. Weeks wore on, the tribe's
          food supply dwindling. Many became sick,
          and everyone was hungry. Then one day a hawk
          dropped something red from its beak into the
          snow. It was a strawberry. Clearly, spring
          had come everywhere else, but it had not
          come to them. The tribe met to discover the
          reason. They talked about things they had
          done and dreams they had had. An old man
          remembered that he had dreamt about a dead
          baby bird. A girl stood up and said that she
          had killed a baby bird with a new slingshot
          the summer before. She had done it without
          thinking, and had forgotten all about it.

          They all walked out on the ice to the
          narrow channel where the river still ran.
          They covered a raft with grass mats for
          the girl to sit on, and they let the
          current carry her away.

          On their way back to the village they felt the sun
          warm on their backs. The sound of trickling
          water began; skunk cabbage appeared through

the softening snow. By night the air smelled
of flowers. That summer the children had
bright eyes again and there was plenty to eat.

One day toward the end of fall, someone saw a
speck on the water upriver floating toward
them. It was the girl sitting on a raft of ice.
By the time she arrived, the whole tribe was
there to greet her.

After that she was called "the one who walks
barefoot in snow," because she did not feel
the cold.

We need to stop living for ourselves.
At a party last week one man said, Think
of all the terrible diseases
people can get!
We might as well help each other!

It is February. Up above Broadway the deep indigo sky
turns again toward night without us.
We are busy getting food and turning on lights,
meeting each other or going home alone.
We wonder whether we know less than the sky knows,
less than the blown sun and its flown-away rock,
or whether we are the only wonderers,
the offspring of action that cannot doubt.

One day I sat in the Cathedral chapel until the sun
changed sides. The tours came through behind me,
a new guide's voice echoing every hour.
"The length of two football fields," they would say.
Someone sat behind me for a long time,
a young man I thought, though I never looked.
He left his prayer book open to this:
The sea is Your way.
Your path is in the great waters,
And Your footsteps are not known.

cont'd

157

Some nights, late, the children long in bed,
as thoughts get longer, and my sentences,
and motives multiply, and the ones I've betrayed
are again betrayed, the newspaper visions
gather behind me. Mistakes penetrate
the veins of the earth.
A bomb is as close as a faulty boiler.
Flame-teasing wind wanders the streets
and the ambulance comes slowly.
I smell the river mixing with the sea,
black under the dark sky.
Wind swaying the street lights,
sing your warnings. Birds with small lungs
and spare lives, smell the danger. Fish
veer from the wrong waters. Old worn balances
in the walls of buildings, exposed wires
about to burn, let one accident
not happen tonight. Hands of the not yet
criminal, let one crime not be
in the paper tomorrow. I think of
my friend Tom, a light sleeper
who is always calling the police.
Smell smoke tonight before it's too late!
Hear a fight starting up and call the police!
Worry and friendliness bungle along. Perhaps
someone in bare feet
pads toward the telephone.

Layle Silbert / photo

David Mura

THE SURVIVOR

for Kinzo Nishida and Hiroshima

Tonight at the harbor
You watched a scarred fisherman
Cleaning his catch, scales like
Sparks flying from his knife.
He placed the bodies in
Boxes: row on row of eyes
Stared upwards, astonished
At their first glimpse of sky.
As blood flecks stained his fingers,
You recalled that once, years
Before, you'd told your mother
How a fisherman slit open a
Fish, revealing cat-whisker bones
And a small heart, still beating—
"If you slit me open like that,"
You said, "I'd die."
Lights on the boats began
To trim the stars, and you
Passed this woman who lifted
And lowered her eyes, as if
Facing a strong wind. Her cheeks
Were mottled, healed. That day
The river was leaking flames
And skulls like lilies floated
On the current, you passed a man
Moaning at the roadside—He rose,
Held out his eyeball in his hand.
And everywhere you looked
You saw his pain.
In the rubble, your belly rumbling,
You built a fire, boiled rice,
Did not cry. Now, by the river
Where dandelion seed-puffs
Float like ghosts in the dark,
You pick up their pieces

Which vibrate in your hands
Like alien metal, which blow
Away like confectionary sugar.
Yes, you have come so far.

John Brandi
ANGEL PEAK: A 2ND ROAD SONG

John—

Get good & sick.
Sick of your self, sick of your body
sick at the sight of Peyote.

Vomit.
Vomit masks, attachment, distractions.
Vomit books & paths.

Have visions, dream, confront ghouls.
Look hard enough at the demons & watch them
turn into sheep. Laugh at yourself & become God.

Sleep alone in a place you've always been
afraid to. Realize mortality.
Be reduced to an ear, a shadow speaking
through yourself. Wake with a cough
clear your throat, become a child.

Enjoy the deep questions
even if they have no answers.

Know the requirements of Wisdom:

—to dance at least once in your life
  that the doors of heaven may open
—to make a fool of yourself, completely
—to love, to be eaten, to die
—to become celibate
—to wander, owning nothing
  always open to the poem
—to find yourself, in solitude
—to witness night as a double-star in a stream
—to hear baby birds sleeping in your eaves
—to renew lovemaking, opening your eyes at climax

to all those alphabets you never understood
—to get good & angry
—to grow older with humor & tenderness
—to let go of what you want & watch it
  come to your door without asking
—to use the fire lit by enemies on all sides
  of you to see by
—to realize you inhabit only a small part of the
  body, & to tell others when they want you
  with passion: "don't look for me there"

John—

    Rest well now.
      Don't fight what keeps you awake.
      Rise exhausted & clean.
      Give it back
            everywhere in the world

Tam Lin Neville

GRIEF DANCE FROM A DISTANT PLACE

It is autumn.
While some leaves are falling
there is a moon calling
certain late ones
to bloom

and children's hands
still dance upon the quilt in pairs,
then sleep
or seek upon the stairs
secrets in the reaching night.
Their just-bathed bodies
go blithe about the house—
all autumns unremembered—
until the cold,
the stove cold,
the wood smell,
frightens them
elatedly

and they return.
Their toes, like drops,
like white and tiny marbles,
play away across the floor.

Music in smoke.

Beneath such leaves
even these tears
are casual.

IN THE beginning God created [1] the heavens and the earth; 2. *a* the earth was [2] waste and void; *b* dark-

ness covered the abyss, and the spirit of God was stirring above the waters.

3. God said, *c* "Let there be light,"

and there was light. God saw that the light was good.[3] 4. God separated the light from the darkness, 5. calling the light Day and the darkness Night. And there was evening and morning, the first day.

6. Then God said, "Let there be a firmament in the midst of the waters to divide the waters." And so it was. 7. *d* God made the firmament, dividing the waters that were below the firmament from those that were above it. 8. God called the firmament Heaven. And there was evening and morning, the second day.

9. Then God said, "Let the waters below the heavens be gathered into one place and let the dry land appear." *e* And so it was. 10. God called the dry land Earth and the assembled

waters Seas. And God saw that it was good. 11. Then God said, *f* "Let the earth bring forth vegetation: seed-bearing plants and all kinds of fruit trees that bear fruit containing their seed." And so it was. 12. The earth brought forth vegetation, every kind of seed-bearing plant and all kinds of trees that bear fruit containing their seed. God saw that it was good. 13. And there was evening and morning, the third day.

14. And God said, "Let there be lights [1] in the firmament of the heavens to separate day from night; let them serve as signs and for the fixing of seasons, days and years; 15. let them serve as lights in the firmament of the heavens to shed light upon the earth." So it was. 16. God made the two great lights, *g* the greater light to rule the day and the smaller one to rule the night, and he made the stars. 17. God set them in the firmament of the heavens to shed light upon the earth, 18. to rule the day and the night and to separate the light from the darkness. *h* God saw that it was good. 19. And there was evening and morning, the fourth day.

20. Then God said, "Let the waters abound with life, and above the earth let winged creatures fly below the firmament [2] of the heavens." And so it was. 21. God created the great sea monsters, all kinds of living, swimming creatures with which the waters abound and all kinds of winged birds. God saw that it was good, 22. and God blessed them, saying, "Be fruitful, multiply, and fill the waters of the seas; and let the birds multiply on the earth." 23. And there was evening and morning, the fifth day. 24. God said, "Let the earth bring forth all kinds of living creatures: cattle, crawling creatures and wild animals." And so it was. 25. God made all kinds of wild beasts, every kind of cattle, and every kind of creature crawling on the ground. And God saw that it was good.

26. God said, "Let us make mankind in our image and likeness; [3] and let them have dominion over the fish of the sea, the birds of the air, the cattle, over all the wild animals and every creature that crawls on the earth."

27. God created man in his image. In the image of God he created him. Male and female he created them. *i*

28. Then God blessed them and said to them, "Be fruitful and multiply; *j* fill the earth and subdue it. Have dominion over the fish of the sea, the birds of the air, the cattle and all the animals that crawl on the earth." 29. God also said, "See, I give you every

seed-bearing plant on the earth and every tree which has seed-bearing fruit to be your food. *k* 30. To every wild animal of the earth, to every bird of the air, and to every creature that crawls on the earth and has the breath of life, I give the green plants for food." And so it was. 31. God saw that all he had made was very good. And there was evening and morning, the sixth day. *l*

THUS the heavens and the earth were finished *m* and all their array. *4* 2. On the sixth day God finished

the work he had been doing. And he rested on the seventh day from all the work he had done. *n*

3. God blessed the seventh day and made it holy *o* because on it he rested *l* from all his work of creation.

Peter Payack / collage: photos with text

Hank De Leo / pen & ink

A.D. Winans

AND GOD LOOKED DOWN AND SAW
HIS CHILDREN PLAYING AT AMCHITKA

After it became obvious that the
U.S. had to perfect its anti-missile system and
After it became obvious that
The president was only keeping up with
The Soviet Union's increasing military might
And after it became obvious that
We had to show the U.N.
We meant business after
They double-crossed us and expelled
Taiwan from
The National Assembly
And after it became obvious that
The pushing of the little red button on
The north end of Amchitka island was just
And in the name of Democracy
And after the congress and the senate and
The president and the courts decreed
The honor of this test to help preserve
The balance of power
And after it became obvious that
The Atomic Energy Commission was as
Powerful as the Pentagon
And after all alternatives were explored
And the Sierra Club declared dangerous to
The national security
Then and only then
Did the forces of the A.E.C. gather at
Amchitka in search of peace through terror
And with the eyes of the world on
The greatest power in history
Some man whose name no one recalls pushed
The tiny red button in the quiet
Of a cold November morning from a bunker
North of Amchitka Island and
The entire Aleutian rock rose up out of

The angry sea exploding in huge
White waves that sent rocks tumbling
Down fifty foot cliffs like giant bowling
Balls in search of death while whole
Sections of the earth fell into the sea
Mute tribute to man's creativity
And after it was over
The smiling government men held a press conference
Mocking those who had predicted dire consequences
Pointing to their hour of final destruction
The only immediate, later to be revised,
Damage report:
A few dead birds and one sea otter apparently
Wounded by falling rocks.

No damage they cried to
The emperor geese
The bald headed eagle
The american falcon who was to be blown from
The cliffs
No damage to the salmon the halibut the sole and
The world's largest population of sea lions and
They scoffed at the ecologists who
Had predicted exploding pressures three thousand pounds
Per square inch which was to whip through
The waters like a sonic boom from five miles out to
The coast and
The sea otters were to die from radiation and
Bursting lungs and ruptured eardrums and
Pray tell what happened to the radiation leakage
And the predicted damage to the salmon industry?

Foolish unfounded fears of those who would not
Listen to the learned men of the A.E.C. who told
Us they had taken every possible precaution burying
The bomb six thousand feet in volcanic rock at
A cost of one hundred and eighteen million dollars
And what of the unemployed and poor
The interest of the nation

Comes first

And what of the island itself with its strange
Bleak sort of beauty when
The sun smiles weighed against
The heavy fog and icy rains and sleet storms
And snow with winds that blow eighty miles an
Hour sometimes reaching twice that force

And what better place to demolish
Few people within several hundred miles
No one except wild life sentenced to death
And there is, was, the World War Two memories
Hanging in the air over two thousand
Quonset huts standing as ugly reminders of
The Aleutian Campaign against the Japanese
With burned out wings and broken
Fuselages of World War Two airplanes

But it is over now and the men from the
A.E.C. proudly announce
The world is still here
And this the 237th underground atomic explosion
Since nineteen-sixty-three
Four times stronger than anything yet tested on earth
All for the balance of power
Ten billion pounds of dynamite exploded
To keep those Spartan anti-missiles moving until
Something better comes along
And then the search for a new
Amchitka will go on and the
President and the courts
Partners in crime
Will remember the unfounded
Fears of the ecologists the timid and the young
And A.E.C. shall be granted
The power they need
These government men cloaked in
God-like power who create

Shock waves that produce
Three million degrees heat
The same temperature found on the
Surface of the
Sun
Waiting to push that tiny
Red button again
Like faceless children caught up in
Atari-like fun

Dan Sullivan / photo

Candice Warne
THE DEAD

The moment is deathless: You are just
a girl, surprised at the forbidden cupboard,
the jar already slipping from your hand,
and nothing in your mind but that *you're caught,*
you're caught; your wicked stepmother swoops down
howling with rage around your dumbstruck head.

Your wits went like a town bombed—
whole blocks of memory gone sudden black,
bare wires spitting sparks in the dark raining.
Her voice is the one thing left that's always clear.
Strike a match, and she's here, in full voice:
    "Close the cover,
    close the cover!
    Damn her ashes!
    I'm the mother now!"

You walk down to the lake at 6 a.m.
with Old Sioux, who wants to bum a smoke.
She's all you get for fairy godmother,
stooped, evasive, and needing a cigarette.
The wind frisks you rudely, drags at your dress,
and turns you back toward the home with a cold kiss;
there are no princes here.

At breakfast, when you lift your cigarette,
Stepmother hisses, deep in your ear,
    "Idiot girl!
    Your father was a good Nazi—
    he gassed the whole pack!"
and the nurses look so bewildered at you;
they won't give you another.
You palm your ashes, rub them in your dress.

Her voice, your voice, pushing you

willy-nilly through another day.
What did you do today? or was
that yesterday, the day before, last week,
all the same day, meal, coffee cup, cigarette,
snow, sun, rain, dark all the same day?

Now the sun's gone. Pace, chain smoke,
and after the Late, Late Show,
after the pills have taken you, outside sleep again,
Old Sioux will pay you back the smoke, and sit
as if only to watch night rub the pane.
She knows there are things we have no words for,
that the night does try to show itself to us,
that the dead can make things go hard for the living.

Warren Woessner
LOOKING AT POWER

1. Nuclear Generating Station, Salem, N.J.

Miles away, the dome rises
over the marsh grass
like a huge, dull moon.
We get as far as the Visitor Center
where a pretty girl hands out "Second Sun" buttons
and comic books that say it's safe:
the happy muskrats and fish don't mind hot water
and "trace amounts of radiation."
An exhibit shows us the hard way:
spin a crank and barely light one bulb.
A child shoots a raygun
and a chain reaction spreads out forever
on the screen. We get the message:
anyone can split the atom
and heat up toasters clear to Newark.

2. Power Units 1 and 2, Colstrip, Montana

Custer's men carved their names on Medicine Rock
then died. The Cheyenne knew they would,
and still wedge prayer sticks in the cracks
hoping for rain
or a job, and peace at home in the trailer.
Twenty miles north, the twin stacks
of the power station's boilers shimmer
in the August heat, strobe lights flashing.
We crouch in the shade of Medicine Rock.
Everything else fits in with no room to spare:
jay, magpie, coyote, even a few men
who stayed long enough to learn the rules.
Now the land's stripped for coal
then dumped back in the pits like trash.
This is whiteman's land—
we close wire gates when we leave.

A DANCE CYCLE

Part One

Armed, I walk the Fall-needled trail
And watch green grasshoppers watch.
In this wind, what continents?

Five dead men in an Asian street
Doo-dah   Doo-dah

You, on the long grass, wait
Tongue tongueing thumb, eyes flat

Casualties have been light
Your son
As to disposal of remains

As I scream, your lips, those
Lips, prepare my comfort;
there are bodies everywhere;
My hands on your breasts;
Lumps that were friends.

You would have been proud of him, sir,
As I was.

I sprawl on you, belly sweats mingling,
And I realize I will die.

Part Two

our sense of honour demands

You. For one thing, your hair;
You're graying. It's been a long time.
Waiter! And I have been cruel.

cont'd

it's not the pale moon that excites me

A soldier writing a poem is blown up.
You bring me tea, and we soak cookies,
And I get tea on my poem
And you are getting grayer.
You will not get much grayer.
I have heard the reports.

Part Three
Insolent bulbs, all dirt and water

owing to unforseen

And the rain stopped, and making love in mud
and gassed soldiers heaving
on color television
and I duck.

For thine is the kingdom and the

Yeah   Yeah

We commit his body

The soldier's poem comes down,
All dirt and water, and the insolent bulbs
lift

The all clear is tripped automatically
But there is no one to hear
So it does not make a sound.

Part Four

there's no tomorrow

I have loved you, earth, apple of my eye,
I know all things can be spoiled:
When Hitler heard of France's fall, he danced.

Leningrad has been completely

This medal to you, Daniel Langton,
For saving a dead soldier's poem

Posthumous

It is Summer
And flowers are hot to the touch.

James Bertolino

THIRTEEN WAYS TO LOOK AT LIFE
AFTER REAGAN

1. Torpid remorse

2. Biohazardous sludge futures

3. Fey shoes

4. Bourgeois anthrax

5. The loathesome slime-born

6. Hemorrhoid events

7. Cancerscapes

8. Glow birds

9. Spent hens versus yodel density

10. Weeping in the back rooms
    of oak-favored homes

11. Praise the post-human

12. And the buzzards never return
    to Hinckley, Ohio

13. O to rape a mallard on a sunny day!

Dellas Henke / intaglio print

Daniel Berrigan
BIOGRAPHY

I was born alive on St. Gregory's day, 1921.
I was born dead on Hiroshima day, 1945.

They baptized me in the name of Trinity, shortly after my
first birth.
They baptized me in the name of Trinity, shortly after my
second birth.

The first baptism was, as theologians say, unconditional.
Beyond doubt
I was born alive and kicking. In the name of Trinity I
baptize you,
someone said.
My second baptism was, as theologians say, conditional. If
you are
alive, someone said, I baptize you in the name of Trinity.

My first baptism was of water. Shortly thereafter, I was told,
a fire
in the church in Ely, Minnesota, destroyed all baptismal
records.
Consequently there was need of a second baptism, a
conditional one.
My second baptism was of fire. Like any infant born
Hiroshima day, I
was presumed dead at birth. Thus, some 24 years after
the first
baptism, I was baptized in fire. With a conditional mercy,
a bib-
lical one; If you live, someone said, I baptize you. In the
name of Trinity.

What does it mean to be alive, what does it mean to be dead?
Or to be
twice born? I believe such things can be explained only
by the

living. Or perhaps by the dead. Or it may be—and this
                                    seems
to touch more nearly on the truth—by those who walk
                                    this world
and another, who breathe this air and another, who tell
                                    this
time and some other. Who are, as the apostle says,
                                    unconformed
to this world. Conformed, at home, at ease, only
                                    elsewhere.

In any case. I, who can be considered a casualty of Hiroshima,
                                    can
also be considered twice born on that day. I am marked
                                    now
by the stigma of those fires, set in my flesh, in the name
                                    of
Trinity. Presumably dead, I have nothing to lose to death.
                                    Pre-
sumed living, I have nothing to refuse life. Or so I hope.

David Ray
AN OLD WOODCUT

Strange resemblance beareth
this old woodcut, date 1604
(man sitting inside doorway
of a sick mountain, scrub-trees,
lions, boulders, in which
is presumed to be the Holy Grail)
to the worshipped nuclear plant
that overshadows barns, drops
ash into the cow-milk, disperses
death quietly, wantonly,
in a civilized manner, salt
and pepper of our skies—
and like the Grail defended,
as if in no way involved
with world's whimpering end
(which sends an archaic chill
through my bones that glow)
while in this yellowed woodcut
having to do with an ancient dream
Parsifal and Gawain crawl
on hands and knees like men in prayer
who bruise their knees and suffer
gladly. And from the nest of towers
churr the wisps of harmless clouds
that we too have heard are harmless,
a kind of evidence of dreaming.

Robert Franzini / intaglio print

Terrance Keenan
AFTER THE NEUTRON

I like to think the first one
will not be a looter
since the private things
of a hundred towns
will be so much the same.
No, someone would get to our place
a long time after, someone curious,
a scientist,
someone with enough memory
when finding the front door locked
to go round to the back.

In the mudroom,
with its old beige walls,
he would see the jumble of boots and coats
that are there winter or summer,
with the several odd things
we never found a place for.
The kitchen will look like
we had just finished breakfast
because I am sure it will happen in the morning.

He won't breathe the air we did
but wisely carry his own.
After a tour he may notice the kitchen
the most lived-in room
and our minor flare for colorful clutter.
But he'll be quickly drawn
to the larger houses up the street
and the empty red stone church
crisp against the birdless sky.

Cathy Young Czapla
CONNECTICUT RIVER, JULY 1976

Even before morning
reaches the river, the nervous deer
have slipped back into the brush.
Already speckled trout
are gasping in the fisherman's creel.
His dog is chasing tadpoles
through the shallows.

Before this day is over,
children will run home as always
with skinned knees and wet socks.
Before the light leaves the water,
bathing suits will be drying
on clotheslines all over town again.
Before the deer
come down to drink at the river
tonight, eighty-three thousand gallons
of radioactive water
will have finally reached Long Island.

Cathy Young Czapla
NEXT MISTAKE

In the southern foothills squats
a methane distillery.
Through its tubes pass
fifty-eight cords of prime succulent
hardwood every hour.
A fifty-megawatt wood-fired generator
has a more delicate appetite:
thirty-one cords chipped just so
and dried to a specific moisture content
every hour.

We have lived
beneath this mountain all our lives.
Five hundred and thirty acres
wooded (the thrushes in the maples)
a trout stream
(the minnows and the mayflies)
only two hundred dollars an acre
and enough wood to fuel a city.

For how long?

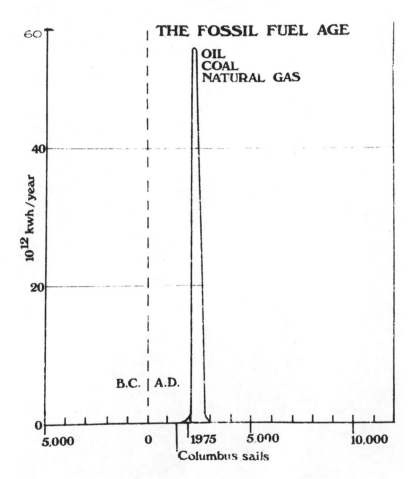

found / fossil fuel graph

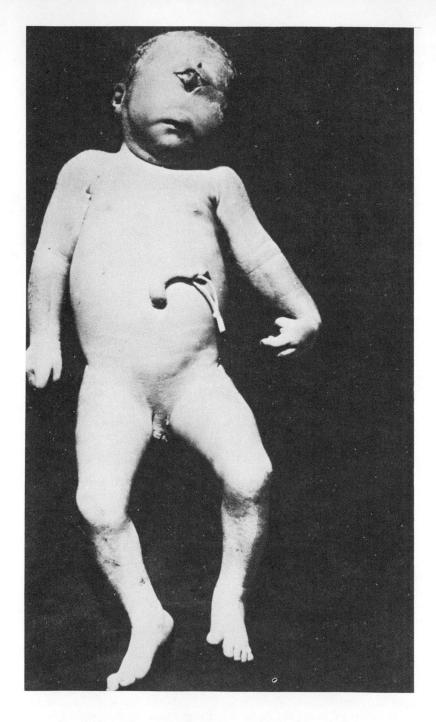

Anonymous / photo
provided by the 1962 Mayor of Hiroshima & Curt Johnson

Michael Clark
THE MAGIC CUP

Although the Roman Empire was, in fact, the most powerful social organization formed before the Dark Ages, it is a supreme irony that its wealth and technology inadvertantly contributed to its demise. The beautifully wrought lead cups that the upperclass could afford slowly poisoned the ruling class, resulting in insanity and ill-health. Though they could see life crumbling about them, they had no way of recognizing lead-poisoning, nor could they suspect that technology could have such adverse side-effects.

—historical fact

NO ONE TALKED about it anymore, but the villagers believed the chalice was magic.

The village in the mountains was so small that there were no newspapers or radios. They were so isolated that there were no newspapers even from other villages or towns. They had forgotten the rest of the world.

In an infrequent, long trip to the Archbishop, their pastor had once been momentarily intrigued by a television newscast. He had heard that this was the age of the atom, but he was very uncertain as to what, exactly, that meant. His village got by well enough even without electricity. Candles, the priest knew, were good enough to light the path to God. So just as he and the villagers forgot the rest of the world, the rest of the world overlooked them.

It is our isolation, the priest said to himself late one night, that leads each member to the altar rail every morning of the week.

He was content that even the archbisop had forgotten him. Fifty-eight years a village pastor. Dying now with the village. He knew he would die here. And the village seemed content to die with him, for although younger members of the parish got married, there seemed to be very few baptisms anymore.

His fiftieth year as village pastor had been celebrated by the entire village. Even the archbishop came that day—the only time he had visited. A high mass was given. His own brother, Francesco, whom he had not seen in thirty years, appeared with a gift of a new chalice—white gold, beautifully wrought with emeralds, rubies, pearls. His own brother, ne'er do well, shepherd, miner, grapepicker, had mined the gold himself, had discovered a lode, a thick vein of it, on the family lands, outside Piombo. That was the same region the ancient Romans had mined for their lavish plates and drinking cups in the fifth century. Francesco had chunks of unrefined ore wrought into a chalice. Aside from that, his claim to the land had brought nothing to the family. Francesco had sat unknowingly on the partially exposed vein for months at a time, while watching his

189

herd of sheep. Then, by accident, one day he discovered the gold. He had mined enough for the chalice, which he then had made in the capital. Before he could return from the high mass celebrating his brother's fifty years, he died. It was rumored that the government fenced in the property and claimed it to pay Francesco's back taxes, but his brother, the pastor of the little village church, had little interest in such things. A government official came to the village one day and had him sign a paper, which the pious priest did not even care to read.

The priest sat in his room with his gnarled fingers grasping the soft, worn leather cover of his prayer book. Lately, the pain in his knuckles had gotten so bad that he had to work at moving the joints to disengage the book. Sometimes he had to remind himself not to pray so long. He sometimes felt that he was too proud of his piety.

Years before, he had heard rumors circulating among the parishioners. They always had talked of his piety. Sometimes he caught a whisper as he would round a street corner. One time a devout parishioner expressed to him in the confessional, her fears about her lack of piety by measuring herself against what she had heard of the Father's self-penance. Yes, he knew that they had talked for years of his all-night vigils in the church, of his horsehair shirts worn during Lent and even through the long, hot summers. The flagellations too. The pastor, he knew, had to lead the flock in piety. But he had to constantly remind himself not to be proud of his suffering.

And now as he had gotten old, the people stopped whispering, and he had the advantage of leaving behind artificial occasions for suffering. Now it came naturally. In the middle of the night he would awake with a pain in his back, like a spear being pushed along his spine from base to neck. The pain of urination would be even worse. Yes, God had blessed him in his old age with bountiful occasions for grace.

The candle was burning low, so he knew from habit that it must be close to three a.m. His eyes watered constantly and stung now, and in the dim light he had to hold the book close to his veiny cheeks and his once aquiline but now bulbous, suppurating nose. He placed the book on the table and slowly worked his fingers away from the cover. Then with a crooked thumb and forefinger, the skin dry, the hand shaking, he slowly pinched out the flame. His lack of coordination made the act slow and painful, but then in the darkness he smiled at the barely perceptible white string of smoke, rising from between his burning, pinched fingers.

He stopped a moment and concentrated on being pious, then padded to the door. He knew that he could not be as meek as the village thought him to be. No. They changed religion into a circus, thought of the spiritual as a magic act. Father is so holy, they said, that his chalice glows in the dark.

They are my children, the pastor thought. Yes, that is it. And I must lead them. He made a resolve to be a better model for them, to sharpen their sense of religion, true faith versus false.

The priest was wearing a white nightgown, slightly soiled and frayed, and walking in the darkness, he seemed an apparition. He padded out the door of the rectory, across the cool courtyard to the church. Now, even walking was an occasion for grace as pain shot up his legs, as if he were constantly walking on a charged electrical plate. But it was only a cobblestone walk sending jolts of feeling through his body. Only at such times as this did he truly feel alive.

The priest understood pain and suffering. When the people suffered and died, he wept as he performed the funeral masses. When they confessed their misdeeds in unintelligible gutterals, he knew that God, the Father, understood their repentance and blessed them. And when every morning the villagers lined the altar rail for communion, the pastor, with gnarled fingers, worked the slivers of wafer from the chalice and then placed them beyond the lips of the communicants, let the hosts slide into their tongueless dark cavities.

And he knew pain at first hand to no small extent.

Diarrhea, bleeding, vomiting, dizziness, he knew were God's way of welcoming him to heaven. Purification involved the casting off of the temporal. Like a sculptor chipping an Adonis from a marble block, God through decay sloughed the body from the soul.

He opened the wooden church door and latched it again behind him. He would set the chalice on the altar and kneel in front of it to pray. Perhaps in an hour his insomnia would pass. It was painful, trying to open the tabernacle door in the dark. Again there would be pain when he would kneel and pray. Perhaps he would stay on his knees several hours, until the people started arriving for morning mass and communion.

They were like children. The other day a vagabond traveller on horseback had passed through with a newspaper published in Piombo. Large black letters, like those that announced the deaths of Popes and Kings, proclaimed, GOLD-URANIUM MINE DISCOVERED. The pastor had shaken his head slowly and smiled to himself when he saw how excited the people were. They marvelled over the texture of the paper, over the fineness of the print. How glad he was that they could not read. Grace was for the simple of spirit.

Carefully, the knobbed hands reached into the tabernacle, cupped the chalice and slowly, slowly withdrew it. He could discern—even with his poor eyesight—the dim glow of the hosts and chalice. In simplicity, he thought, the people see magic in that glow. But it is only God. The ever-present hand of God cradles us in his wisdom and does not forget us. Just a few years before, when he had fingernails and long smooth fingers, those nails and cuticles too would shine as he clasped the cup in the night—back when baptisms were performed and the parishioners had tongues.

Grant Burns
WHAT THE DEAD WANT

THE RAIN is still falling. It makes a vague whimpering noise on the church roof, not the healthy patter of a good spring rain or the rush of an August storm, but a tedious, nagging, incessant and wearying intrusion on the ear.

The air in the church is clammy from the rain. Although it is warm, there is always a shivering within, as though someone has placed a cold hand on one's back. The wooden benches at the back of the church are sticky with humidity; somehow the saturated air brings the years of sweat passed into the wood from the bodies of summertime worshippers back to the surface. Everything one touches feels as though it has just escaped the nervous hands of an overdressed, recently-bereaved penitent. The hymnals in the racks, the flyers announcing the coming week's activities, the programs on which one tries to outline plans for the future during the long stretches of boredom and inertia, all are damp, limp, on the verge of mold.

The electric lights no longer work. Candles once saved for the service now illuminate the far reaches of the church, glimmering pathetically in the great shadow that has come to a permanent rest on the interior. Not even the sun, on days when the rain and clouds dissipate, penetrates the darkness within. The stained glass windows are so deep, so blood-like in their color that they effectively stop all but a few feeble beams from entering. When the sun shines and creates a glow of dark intensity in the stained glass, the church seems even darker than when lit only by candles. There is a mocking quality in the sunlit glass that leads one to avoid looking at it. As monotonous as the rain has become, it is almost preferable to the sun.

No one enjoys the sun anymore.

An old key-wound clock hangs on the back wall of the church. It looks like a prop from a Hollywood western, the clock in "High Noon" ticking off the hours and minutes before the sheriff must face the bad men alone on the city streets. The brass pendulum swings back and forth, the long black hands turn slowly around the white face with its black numerals now fading into gray. Time still matters, and the minister himself tends to the winding of the clock.

I miss the old weather. I miss its changes. In the past, at this time of year, I might go to bed after a shirtsleeve walk in the spring night, then wake up to find snow falling, covering the ground, slicking the streets. In a few hours the snow might burn away, the new season reasserting itself with the sunrise. Now it is the same, every day. The temperature has not varied more than ten degrees in the last eight months. The sun comes through a few days each month, but there has not been a wholly clear day in over a year. The rain is rotting everything.

192

I surprise myself by how often I refer to time and the future. Years and months and hours, seasons and days, the necessities to accomodate with the assumption that by accomodating them we will insure a future—in this daily drudgery of colorless uniformity, in the grinding routine that has settled upon us.

The past sometimes seems as immediate as anything now happening. Even dreams are hard to tell from reality. They visit me with great clarity, and endure well beyond waking. I do not know if others experience these dreams; we seldom talk anymore about anything but the necessary: obtaining food, worship, carrying out the dead. I suspect, though, that such dreams of clarity are common, provoked by excessive fatigue, boredom, lack of faith in the future, physiological longing. In my own dreams I explore the past as if it still held possibilities for a future yet to come. The future has come, and the possibilities are no longer with us. I dream of escape, not surprising considering the difficulty one meets now in a journey of a few miles.

I dreamed last night that I walked into a travel agency near my old place of work to answer a newspaper advertisement soliciting a partner to set out on an expedition through Australia and neighboring islands. The travel agent was my wife, but she did not recognize me. I questioned her closely about her position, but nothing she said indicated she knew who she was.

No one is what anyone was before, except for the priests and the legal authorities. Some physicians still practice. Some believe that some day it will all be as it was. I would rather be dead.

Words come slowly. Time goes quickly. We struggle in the current, looking for a ledge or a snag to grasp until we have found the right words for everything we wanted to say, but the current is too fast and we are swept away, swept away like the dead leaves fallen from overhanging branches into a mad river. The flow pulls us along. Everything we cling to breaks away and we roar on to oblivion.

All my dreams have come true, and were true even before I dreamed them. My dreams filled me with dread, yet I still cannot believe that everything is inevitable. I am a fool.

I have sat on old sofas with plaintive music plying my senses, while out in the darkness just beyond the wall the immigrants beat their drums in protest of their mistreatment. I cannot help them. The noise from the perimeter is overpowering, though barely perceptible. I must speak to the minister about this. I am convinced that he will have something to say.

Everything is getting away, flying to endless voids, while self-assured men and women even now pursue honor and wealth among their admiring and jealous peerage.

I see the woman I loved combing her hair over one shoulder as she looks at herself in a mirror. I see her eyes in the glass looking back at me and I see her smile reflected in the glass and hear her voice reflected by the ceramic tile walls, and after I have shut the door, still I hear her, and after I have touched her hand, still I hold her without knowledge or desire. She is dead but she is with me, and I cannot choose between a lie I detest and the life I would save.

I am due soon at the carrying-out. It is my turn.

Now it is night and the rain continues its dreary distant noise on the church roof. Nightmares plague me tonight. I have heard that if I face the street and listen for the noises from the perimeter, I will know the wants of the dead.

I am afraid to be awake.

Randall W. Scholes / pen & ink

Curt Johnson
OUR NUCLEAR FUTURE

written in 1959

RADIATION does not hurt. We cannot see it, hear it, smell it, taste it or feel it. Nature has given us no way to detect it. Yet if radiation penetrates the body in any amount, no matter how small, it damages.

Radiation damage may show itself as cancer or as leukemia or as premature aging in the irradiated individual. Or it may show itself as mutations in children born dead or physically deformed or mentally defective. The consequences of radiation damage are ugly, but once man learned how to fission the nucleus of an atom—an act which produces radiation—it became certain that he would experience them to an increasing extent.

Man-made radiation is a comparatively new factor in the human environment. It has existed in quantity only since the first nuclear weapon explosion in 1945. We do not know exactly how many human beings have so far been harmed to an appreciable degree by man-made radiation, but the most optimistic estimates cite totals in the millions. We do know that the agents of this damage are not reversible. Radioactive dust from the nuclear explosions of the past 15 years is in the soil now and it will continue to fall from the sky for many years to come—even if there are no further weapons tests.

Strontium-90, one of the chief agents of radiation damage, did not exist on earth before the advent of the atomic age. Today it is everywhere on earth, in the sea and sky, and in the body of every living thing.

Fallout deposits Sr-90 on earth where it is taken up by plants. The plants are eaten by humans or by farm animals, or the animals or their products (such as milk) are consumed by humans and then, because Sr-90 is chemically similar to calcium, it is deposited in the bone, where it remains for many years (its average life is 40 years), giving off its energy as beta rays.

Beta rays from a radioactive element such as Sr-90 ionize atoms of the bone and can eventually cause bone cancer or leukemia. The clinical course of bone cancer usually begins some 5 or 20 years after deposit of the radioactive element. The symptoms are boring, burning or knifelike pains, or spontaneous fractures, followed by malignant tumor formation, with death usually occurring from one to five years after the onset of symptoms. Like other types of cancer, bone cancer is a lingering and intensely painful disease.

The bones of children are growing and take up more calcium, and therefore more strontium-90, than adults'. Moreover, Sr-90 does not settle uniformly in a child's bones, but in small pockets at the centers of growth. In tests on animals, such pockets were found to be 50 times more radioactive than the surrounding bone and in each case these hot pockets were the site of malignant tumor origin.

Only a fraction of the Sr-90 now in the skies has fallen and only a fraction of what has fallen has gotten into human bones. Present estimates are that within five years the average amount of Sr-90 in the average young child's bones will be three times what it is today, that 10 percent of our children will have six times what they have today, and that 1 percent will have 15 times today's level.

But these are only estimates of levels. They do not tell us how many cases of bone cancer or leukemia these levels will cause. Scientists will guess that within a generation Sr-90 may have caused roughly 150,000 cases of bone cancer or leukemia. But they do not hesitate to add that the true effects might easily be 10 times larger.

The chief source of man-made radiation today is fallout from weapons tests. Tomorrow the chief source may be contamination from nuclear power plant reactors, for in addition to generating electricity these plants produce radioactive wastes. These wastes accumulate; they cannot be destroyed. By the time the nuclear power program of the U.S. is well underway, we will be producing over 50 million gallons of dangerous, high-level wastes each year. By the end of this century we will have accumulated almost *2½ billion* gallons.

At present we discharge most of our radioactive nuclear wastes into rivers, streams and sewers. The rest we put into drums and dump into the sea—where, some scientists believe, gases will form and explode the drums; bury it in the ground—where it may then seep into subterranean streams; or let it soak away into the soil.

Because of increasing radioactive contamination of the sea and atmosphere, many of the experiments necessary to determine how large quantities of radioactive wastes can be safely disposed of—if they can be—will be impossible within 10 to 15 years. Yet research into the disposal problem is almost nonexistent.

So far our handling of radioactive wastes parallels our earlier experience with the disposal of industrial and human wastes. Then, inadequate knowledge, special interest and unfounded optimism ignored the problem, and wastes were indiscriminately sluiced into inland and coastal waters. Many of the waters so used have been unable to purify themselves and—lacking the necessary, expensive treatment—remain poisoned and a menace. There is *no* treatment that will reverse an ill-considered disposal of radioactive wastes.

Though we may be sure that nuclear power installations will be carefully engineered and maintained, accidental discharge of waste into the atmosphere is bound to occur. Already there have been mishaps at installations in the U.S., in Canada and in England. And by the end of this century—in only 40 years—the discharge of just 1 percent of the world-wide

Sr-90 inventory that could then exist would contaminate the surface of
the entire earth.

The least of the worries connected with our nuclear future would
seem to be the ultimate horror, the use of nuclear weapons in war. If a
nuclear war comes, most of the world's population will die almost immediately and the genetic and physical damage to the survivors will be
disastrous as far as the future of mankind is concerned.

The chief of our worries may well be the risk we run in conducting
even our present, peace-limited nuclear experimentation. Because of past
nuclear explosions, for example, bread picked at random from the
shelves of a supermarket is found to be four times as radioactive as is
"safe." Because of past explosions, midwest-grown grain samples register
unexpectedly high levels of radioactivity—as much as 6 to 10 times the
officially set maximums. Because of past explosions, nationwide tests reveal a continuing steep rise in the radioactive contamination of U.S.
milk. The consequences of these levels are defective and deformed in-
fants and bone cancer and leukemia victims..

Are we proceeding with due caution? Have we established careful con-
trols? Do we, in fact, know enough about the hazards of nuclear experimentation to proceed at all? For if an environment is modified beyond
the tolerance of its population, migration or death is certain. Radiation
from nuclear experimentation is modifying our entire planet's environment, and we do not know enough to set intelligent limits to this modi-
fication. If it proceeds too far, there is no place for us to go.

Most scientists admit that they do not yet have enough data to speak
on the dangers involved, and the people who do speak on these dangers—
military men, politicians, diplomats—for the most part have the same
special interest that in the U.S. has repeatedly prompted the Atomic Energy Commission to make statements of unfounded optimism.

The AEC has had the dual responsibility of developing weapons and
evaluating radiation hazards. It has concentrated on the first responsibility and ignored the second—ignored it so completely that we know al
most nothing of practical value about the extent of the dangers of radiation or about protection from them. (The AEC's approach to the second
responsibility may be inferred from the title it gave to a study it commissioned on the effects of fallout: "Project Sunshine.") The AEC has
withheld information on fallout and it has minimized its hazards, sometimes through ignorance, so as to reassure and soothe the public. It has
never publicly discussed—seriously and in detail—the arguments advanced
against continued weapons testing and it has prevented scientists from
revealing potential dangers. It virtually admits it does not know enough
to evaluate radiation hazards. For example, answering a query about the
procedures involved in measuring fallout from bomb tests, an AEC
spokesman responded, "We will know about it when it comes down...."

Granted that the decision to continue or discontinue experimentation in nuclear energy applications involves military, political and economic considerations, surely the most important consideration is whether we have the right to risk the health and lives of our own and future generations when we do not know the extent of the risk we are taking.

This last consideration is one about which we would do well to make inquiry. In a democratic society the premise is that the individual has the final responsibility for decisions and that he is entitled to all the information public officials can provide. It is a mistake to assume that we must make decisions on such a risk, or permit others to make them for us, until we know all that is or may be involved.

The history of tolerance levels for radiation is one of periodic and drastic downward revision. If we were to find 15 years from now that the people of the world had received too much radiation, or would eventually receive too much from the man-made radioactivity then existing, it would be too late to do anything about it. The earth and its inhabitants would be incurably tainted.

What *are* the chronic, long-term effects of radiation on humans? No one knows. But until the scientists are able to tell the authorities more about these effects, and until the authorities present this information to us, we might reasonably make a demand for a permanent discontinuance of nuclear testing and for a redirection of our efforts toward ways of reducing—if we can—the harmful effects from those radioactive contaminants we already have with us. Even in an age such as ours—or perhaps especially in an age such as ours—such common sense would seem to be urgently called for.

The Director of the AEC's Division of Biology and Medicine recently [1959] stated that "no one so far as we are aware proposes that there should be no exposure to man-made sources of radiation."

Until the authorities know more, and tell us, here is such a proposal.

N O T I C E

OFFICE OF CIVILIAN DEFENSE
WASHINGTON D.C.

**INSTRUCTION TO PATRONS ON PREMISES
IN CASE OF NUCLEAR BOMB ATTACK:**

<u>**UPON THE FIRST WARNING:**</u>

1) STAY CLEAR OF ALL WINDOWS.
2) KEEP HANDS FREE OF GLASSES, BOTTLES, CIGARETTES, ETC.
3) STAND AWAY FROM BAR, TABLES, ORCHESTRA, EQUIPMENT AND FURNITURE.
4) LOOSEN NECKTIE, UNBUTTON COAT AND ANY OTHER RESTRICTIVE CLOTHING.
5) REMOVE GLASSES, EMPTY POCKETS OF ALL SHARP OBJECTS SUCH AS PENS, PENCILS, ETC.
6) IMMEDIATELY UPON SEEING THE BRILLIANT FLASH OF NUCLEAR EXPLOSION, BEND OVER AND PLACE YOUR HEAD FIRMLY BETWEEN YOUR LEGS.
7) THEN KISS YOUR ASS GOODBYE.

Morty Sklar / found words, with "transfer" visuals

Contributor notes follow.

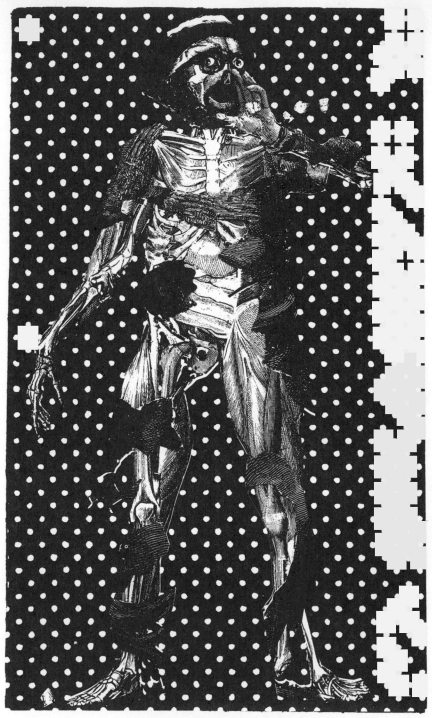

Carlo Pittore / pen & brush & ink

Jimmy Santiago Baca's latest book of poems, from Curbstone Press in Connecticut, is *What's Happening*.

Daniel Berrigan. No current biographical information provided.

James Bertolino has eight books of poems out, the most recent titled, *New And Selected Poems* (Carnegie Mellon, 1978) and *Are You Tough Enough For The Eighties?* (New Rivers Press, 1979). He co-edits the *Cincinnati Poetry Review* and *Eureka Review*.

John Brandi's *The Cowboy From Phantom Banks* (type of writing not given) is from Floating Island. His collected poems, *That Back Road In*, is from Wingbow Press. His most recent poetry book, from Toothpaste Press, is titled, *Rite For The Beautification Of All Beings*.

Joseph Bruchac's most recent publications include a novel, *The Dreams Of Jesse Brown* (Cold Mountain Press) and a collection of poems, *Translator's Son* (Cross-Cultural Communications Press). He is the editor of The Greenfield Review Press and a member of NAMI (National Association of Metis Indians).

Dennis Brutus recently (September 11, 1983) wrote, "This week we had the great joy of hearing [a judge] order in immigration court that I be given political asylum." Brutus had been teaching at Northwestern for quite some time, but was facing deportation to South Africa due to a "technicality." He and others felt his life would be in jeopardy if he were deported.

Byron Burford's artwork (mostly paintings) have been shown in many solo and group and invitational exhibitions. His work is collected at the Walker Art Center (Minneapolis), the San Francisco Museum of Modern Art, the Des Moines Art Center, Queens University (Ontario) and many other places.

Grant Burns: "I was born two years after the Hiroshima and Nagasaki bombings. Like others my age or younger, I cannot remember a time in my life when we could trust that the world would survive the day to come." Burns co-edits, with Casey Hill, *New Pages: News And Reviews Of The Progressive Book Trade*.

Robert M. Chute's most recent book of poetry is *Thirteen Moons/Treize Lunes*, from Penumbra Press (Ontario). He is a professor of biology and Chairman of the Division of Science and Mathematics at Bates College. He founded and edited *The Small Pond* magazine.

Michael Clark's fiction has appeared in *The Yale Literary Magazine, Ann*

Arbor Review, The Madison Review and other places. He's currently teaching creative writing at Widener College, is married and "teaching my son Andrew how to spell."

Robert Creeley's newest publications are: *The Collected Poems Of Robert Creeley, 1945-1975*, from the University of California Press, 1982, and *A Calendar* (poems, on a calendar) from Toothpaste Press, 1983.

Cathy Young Czapla's poetry chapbook from Samisdat is titled, *Genetic Memories*. She's also published in *image, Blackjack* and *New Kauri*.

Hank De Leo's drawings have appeared in *The New York Times*, McGraw-Hill books, *The Progressive* and elsewhere.

Don Dolan's book of drawings, *The Last Days Of The American Dream*, is from The Fault Press (Calif.).

W.D. Ehrhart's "non-fiction novel," *Vietnam-Perkasie: The Long Road Out And Back*, was published by McFarland & Co. He has four collections of poetry, among them: *The Samisdat Poems* (Samisdat Press) and *The Awkward Silence* (Northwoods Press).

Sally Fisher's adaptation of a Japanese fairy tale, *The Tale Of The Shining Princess*, was published by The Metropolitan Museum of Art and Viking. Her book of poems, *Eleven Ghazals*, was published by Katz Howans Press.

Hugh Fox's *The Guernica Cycle: The Year Franco Died* ("1,200 pages of Spanish Journal excerpted down to 100 pages") was published by Cherry Valley Editions, fall 1983. He's currently gathering his prose pieces from the 1960s and 1970s for a book called *The Invisible Generation*.

Robert Franzini. No biographical information provided.

Diane Glancy has poems in the Greenfield Review Press' *Songs From This Earth On Turtle's Back* (1983). A chapbook of her American Indian poetry is scheduled for publication in 1984 by *Blue Cloud Quarterly*.

James Grabill has a book of poetry from Lynx House Press, titled *To Other Beings*, and has published poetry in *kayak, Greenfield Review, Jazz* and *Mississippi Mud*.

Chael Graham, translator of the Prevert poem here, is Project Director at the Coordinating Council of Literary Magazines.

Roger Greenwald, translator of the Jacobsen poems here, recently received a Translation Center Award for Jacobsen's poems. He is founder and editor of *Writ* magazine.

Tom Hansen teaches at Northern State College in Aberdeen, South Dakota. He's been publishing poetry and prose for ten years.

Dellas Henke began painting in Rochester, New York, where he was born and raised, "as often as possible and almost as far back as I can remember." He teaches printmaking at Grand Valley State College in Michigan.

David Hilton lives in Baltimore and teaches English at Anne Arundel Community College. He has two books of poetry: *Huladance* (Crossing Press) and *The Candleflame* (Toothpaste Press). He's a contributing editor for *Abraxas*, and recently published reviews in *Exquisite Corpse*.

Will Inman works with retarded people in Tucson. He recently published long poems in *Pembroke Magazine* and *Ironwood*. He's editor of *New Kauri*, a Spanish-English poetry magazine.

Rolf Jacobsen has published eleven books of poetry since 1933 (and five collections from them), the most recent being *Tenk pa noe annet* (*Think About Something Else*) in 1979. He won the Norwegian Critics' Prize in 1958.

Curt Johnson has had four novels and fifty short stories published (as of July 1981; details not provided), and has been the editor of December Press and magazine for twenty-one years.

Terrance Keenan: From 1972-1979 he was "the only small press bookseller in rural central New York." His book of poems, *Cambros*, was published by Zephyr Press (San Diego) in 1979. His poems have been anthologized in the *Ardis Anthology Of New American Poetry, On Turtle's Back* and *The Apple Anthology*.

Jascha Kessler's most recent book is a translation from the Serbo-Croatian of Grozdana Olujic titled *Rose Of Mother-Of-Pearl: Three Fairy Tales*, published by Toothpaste Press, 1983.

Hayashi Kyoko's story is, as one would suspect in reading it, autobiographical. It was first published in Japan, where it was awarded the Akutagawa Prize. She has also published a novel and several collections of short stories.

Daniel Langton. No biographical information provided.

Cleveland Latham is Director of College Guidance at The McCallie School, a boarding school for boys. He's published fiction and poetry in *Xavier Review, American Man* and *Uwharrie Review*, as well as other little magazines.

Eugene McCarthy, former Senator from Minnesota, is also a poet.

Brown Miller has eight books of poetry out, the latest of which is *Hiroshima Flows Through Us*, from Cherry Valley Editions, 1977. He's poetry editor of the *San Francisco Review Of Books*.

David Mura is a *sansei*, a third generation Japanese-American. His poems have appeared in *The American Poetry Review, The Chowder Review, Quarry, The Asian-American Poetry Anthology* and *Brother Songs*.

Tam Lin Neville: "I try (unsuccessfully) to thread my way through the 'pretentious multiplicity' (Rilke) that surrounds me."

D. Nurkse has recent work in *The California Quarterly* and *Confrontation*.

William Oandasan has a book of poems titled *A Branch Of California Redwood* (no publisher given), and is editor of the *American Indian Culture And Research Journal* and *A*, a journal of contemporary literature.

Lee Patton has taught creative writing, film and literature at Douglas County High School for the past nine years.

Peter Payack is a poet, "environmental artist," editor of *Phone-A-Poem* in Cambridge/Boston, and an inventor of the Stonehenge Watch and other things. His latest books are, *The Growth Of Human Ideas* (Vehicle Press, 1981) and *Rainbow Bridges* (Samisdat Press, 1980). He's published in *Oink!, The Paris Review, The New York Times, Reader's Digest, Asimov's Science Fiction Magazine, The Ecologist, Rolling Stone* and many other places, in the U.S. and abroad.

Marge Piercy's most recent book of poetry is *Stone, Paper, Knife* (Knopf, 1983). Her collection of essays, mostly about poetry, *Parti-Colored Blocks For A Quilt* was published by Arbor Press, 1983. Her new novel, *Fly Away Home* is from Summit Press (winter 1983).

Carlo Pittore: Only biographical note received is a postcard from Rome —"Am painting and trying to learn enough to make a contribution—not very easy—but *very* exciting, eh?" Pittore is the editor/publisher of the art press, Pittore Euforico.

Jacques Prevert's book of poems, *Paroles*, first published in France in 1946, was almost immediately reprinted. By 1952 there were 200,000 copies in print.

Margaret Randall lives in Nicaragua with her four children and "the dream of a just world." Her newest book is *From Witness To Struggle: Christians In The Nicaraguan Revolution*. Other books: *Cuban Women Now, Spirit Of The People: Women In Vietnam, Sandino's Daughters, Inside The Nicaraguan Revolution: The Story Of Doris Maria*, and more.

David Ray's newest book of poems, *The Touched Life*, was published by The Scarecrow Press in 1982. He's the editor of *New Letters*, which published its *Reader I* in 1983.

Helen Redman's artwork has been shown in twenty one-person shows and in numerous juried and invitational exhibitions throughout this country and in France. She's the Grand Prize winner of the 1982 Children's Diabetes Art Competition.

Gay Rogers, after teaching printmaking for five years, moved to a warehouse in Houston, Texas, to set up a print shop and become a full time artist. Her work is in twenty-eight permanent collections.

William Pitt Root. No biographical note received.

Randall W. Scholes is an illuminator of Small Press literature. He's contributed to *25 Minnesota Poets*, numbers 1 & 2, *Brother Songs*, and *To See A Thing*, by Keith Gunderson. He's the art director for *Milkweed Chronicle*.

Hillel Schwartz' poem, published here, is part of a long series of poems called "Some Local Aristocracy," twenty of which have been published in various journals. He finished a novel, *New Blue God*, and a play, "American Domestic Flights." He's a dancer, choreographer, historian and professor of English.

Kyoko Selden, Hyashi Kyoko's translator, is a poet, and a teacher specializing in contemporary Japanese and comparative literature. She is presently working on a volume on the literature of the atomic bomb.

Grace Shinell is a researcher and zen student, as well as a writer. She's presently working on a satirical novel, a section of which appears in this book.

Layle Silbert works as a free-lance photographer specializing in writers. Her book of poems, *Making A Baby In Union Park Chicago* was published by Downtown Poets in 1983.

Morty Sklar, editor/publisher of The Spirit That Moves Us Press, has had his poems anthologized in *A to Z: 200 Contemporary American Poets* (Swallow Press/Ohio University Press, 1981), *Brother Songs: A Male Anthology Of Poetry* (Holy Cow! Press, 1979) and in *Poesia Tambem E Literatura*, contemporary North American poetry (Ilha Do Desterro, Brazil, 1979).

Floyd Skloot has a book of poems, *Rough Edges*, from Chowder Chapbooks, 1979. He's manager of programming for the Illinois Capital Development Board.

Gary Snyder's *Axe Handles*, published in 1983 by North Point Press, is his first collection of new poems since *Turtle Island*, for which he was awarded the Pulitzer Prize in 1974.

William Stafford's latest book, *Segues* (a correspondence in poetry, with Marvin Bell) is from David Godine. Other recent books are from West Coast Poetry Review Press, BOA Editions, and Copper Canyon Press.

Robert Stewart edited *Voices From The Interior: Poets Of Missouri* for BkMk Press, 1983.

Dan Sullivan's photograph is from a series of fifteen images called Backways. "In the series I tried to record the forgotten fragments/artifacts of a culture that had lost touch with its soul." His photographs have appeared in *Photographer's Forum's Best Of Photography Annuals Of 1981 and 1982.*

Judith Waring started writing seriously "after a short, early dabbling in a biology career and a long stretch of motherhood (including fifteen years of preschoolers)."

Candice Warne has published poems in *Sou'wester, Hiram Poetry Review, Mickle Street Review* and other places. She's completing work on a collection of apocalypse/post apocalypse dreams, which has a positive perspective.

A.D. Winans: "In the '50s—returned from Panama to share in the declining days of the 'beat' generation. . . In the '70s—founded *Second Coming* magazine and press." He has ten books of poetry out, and has edited several anthologies, including *19 + 1: An Anthology Of San Francisco Poetry*, most recently, and was included in, most recently, *Terpentin On The Rocks: An Anthology Of Contemporary American Poets*, published in Germany.

Warren Woessner's most recent book of poems is *No Hiding Place* (Spoon River Press). He edits reviews for *Abraxas*. He recently moved to New York City from Madison, Wisconsin.

Yamahata Yosuke. Nothing is known to us of this photographer whose photograph, published here, first appeared in *Days To Remember.*